MUDRAS for ASTROLOGICAL SIGNS

Healing Yoga Hand Postures for the ZODIAC

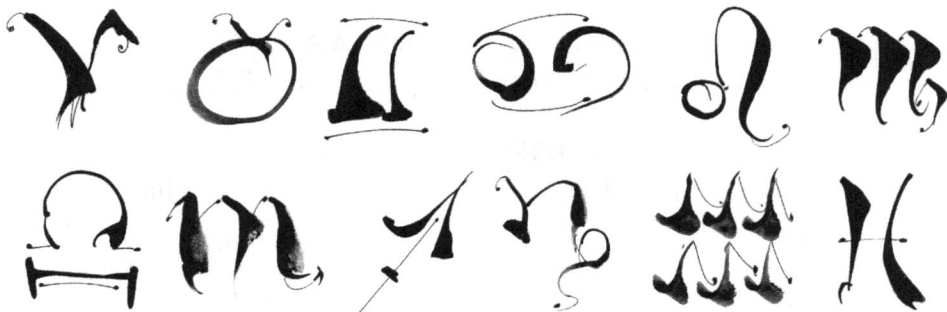

By Sabrina Mesko

HEALING MUDRAS
Yoga for Your Hands
Random House - Original edition

POWER MUDRAS
Yoga Hand Postures for Women
Random House - Original edition

MUDRA - Gestures of POWER
DVD - Sounds True

CHAKRA MUDRAS DVD set
HAND YOGA for Vitality, Creativity and Success
HAND YOGA for Concentration, Love and Longevity

HEALING MUDRAS
Yoga for Your Hands - New Edition

HEALING MUDRAS - New Edition in full color:
Healing Mudras I. ~ For Your Body
Healing Mudras II. ~ For Your Mind
Healing Mudras III. ~ For Your Soul

POWER MUDRAS
Yoga Hand Postures for Women - New Edition

MUDRA THERAPY
Hand Yoga for Pain Management and Conquering Illness

YOGA MIND
45 Meditations for Inner Peace, Prosperity and Protection

MUDRAS for ASTROLOGICAL SIGNS
Volumes I. ~ XII.

MUDRAS for ARIES, TAURUS, GEMINI, CANCER, LEO, VIRGO, LIBRA, SCORPIO, SAGITTARIUS, CAPRICORN, AQUARIUS, PISCES
12 Book Series

LOVE MUDRAS
Hand Yoga for Two

MUDRAS AND CRYSTALS
The Alchemy of Energy Protection

MUDRAS
for ASTROLOGICAL SIGNS

by

Sabrina Mesko Ph.D.H.

MUDRA HANDS
PUBLISHING

The material contained in this book has been written for informational purposes
and is not intended as a substitute for medical advice,
nor is it intended to diagnose, treat, cure, or prevent disease.
If you have a medical issue or illness, consult a qualified physician.

A MUDRA Hands™ Book
Published by Mudra Hands Publishing

Copyright © 2016 Sabrina Mesko

Cover and interior Photography by Mara
Symbol Design Kiar Mesko
Animal Photography Sabrina Mesko
Cover and interior book design by Sabrina Mesko
Printed in the United States of America

First MUDRA Hands Publishing Edition
December 2016

Manufactured in the United States of America

ISBN-13: 978 - 0692823958

ISBN-10: 0692823956

All rights reserved. No part of this book may be reproduced or transmitted in any
form or by any means, electronic or mechanical, including photocopying,
recording, or by any information storage and retrieval system,
without the prior written permission from the Publisher.

*May the Stars shine upon You
with Blessings of Eternal Love...*

TABLE OF CONTENTS

INTRODUCTION 16

PART 1 ~ Instructions for Practice 19
What are Mudras? 20
How do Mudras work? 20
Breath Control 21
Chakras 21
Nadis 23
Your Hands and the Cosmos 24
Mantra 24
About Astrology 25
Your Sun Sig 25
Your Rising Sign 26
How to use this book 26

PART 2 ~ Mudra Sets 27
ARIES 28
MUDRAS for TRANSCENDING CHALLENGES 30
MUDRA of Developing Meditation 31
MUDRA for Taking You Out of Danger 32
MUDRA for Third Chakra 33
MUDRAS for Your HEALTH AND BEAUTY 34
MUDRA for Transcending Anger and Headache 35
MUDRA for Emotional Balance 36
MUDRA for Calming Your Mind 37
MUDRAS for LOVE 38
MUDRA to Open Your Heart 39
MUDRA for Sixth Chakra - Truth 40
MUDRA of Two Hearts 41
MUDRAS for SUCCESS 42
MUDRA for Guidance 43
MUDRA for Patience 44
MUDRA for Efficiency 45

TAURUS 46
MUDRAS for TRANSCENDING CHALLENGES............................48
MUDRA of Powerful Insight...49
MUDRA for Meditation of Change...50
MUDRA for Evoking Inner Strength..51
MUDRAS for Your HEALTH AND BEAUTY.......................................52
MUDRA for Powerful Voice 53
MUDRA of Recharging..54
MUDRA for Rejuvenation 55
MUDRAS for LOVE 56
MUDRA for Higher Consciousness...57
MUDRA of Truth 58
MUDRA for Trust 59
MUDRAS for SUCCESS 60
MUDRA for a Sharp Mind 61
MUDRA for Releasing Negative Emotions 62
MUDRA for Inner Integrity..63

GEMINI 64
MUDRAS for TRANSCENDING CHALLENGES............................66
MUDRA for Contentment..67
MUDRA for Relaxation and Joy 68
MUDRA for Protection 69
MUDRAS for Your HEALTH AND BEAUTY.......................................70
MUDRA for Uplifting Your Heart 71
MUDRA for Diminishing Worries 72
MUDRA for Healthy Breast 73
MUDRAS for LOVE 74
MUDRA of Two Hearts 75
MUDRA for Healing Your Heart Chakra 76
MUDRA of Right Speech 77
MUDRAS for SUCCESS 78
MUDRA for Self-Confidence 79
MUDRA for Powerful Insight 80
MUDRA for Sharp Mind 81

CANCER 81
MUDRAS for TRANSCENDING CHALLENGES 84
MUDRA for Inner Security 85
MUDRA for Self-Confidence 86
MUDRA for Diminishing Worries 87
MUDRAS for Your HEALTH AND BEAUTY 88
MUDRA for Emotional Balance 89
MUDRA for Strong Nerves 90
MUDRA for Removing Depression 91
MUDRAS for LOVE 92
MUDRA for Releasing Guilt 93
MUDRA for Happiness 94
MUDRA of Preventing Stress 95
MUDRAS for SUCCESS 96
MUDRA for Prosperity 97
MUDRA for a Calm Mind 98
MUDRA for Mental Balance 99

LEO 100
MUDRAS for TRANSCENDING CHALLENGES 102
MUDRA for Receiving God's Law 103
MUDRA for Readjusting your Perception 104
MUDRA for Inner Integrity 105
MUDRAS for Your HEALTH AND BEAUTY 106
MUDRA for Healthy Breast and Heart 107
MUDRA for Activating Lower Chakras 108
MUDRA for Middle Spine 109
MUDRAS for LOVE 110
MUDRA for Opening Your Heart 111
MUDRA for Compassion 112
MUDRA of Uplifting Your Heart 113
MUDRAS for SUCCESS 114
MUDRA for Mental Balance 115
MUDRA for Powerful Insight 116
MUDRA for Better Communication 117

VIRGO 118
MUDRAS for TRANSCENDING CHALLENGES 120
MUDRA for Compassion 121
MUDRA for Releasing Negativity 122
MUDRA for Relaxation and Joy 123
MUDRAS for Your HEALTH AND BEAUTY 124
MUDRA for Second Chakra 125
MUDRA for Strong Nerves 126
MUDRA for Releasing Anxiety 127
MUDRAS for LOVE 128
MUDRA for Opening Your Heart 129
MUDRA for Love 130
MUDRA of Guidance 131
MUDRAS for SUCCESS 132
MUDRA for Self-Confidence 133
MUDRA for Creativity 134
MUDRA for Powerful Insight 135

LIBRA 136
MUDRAS for TRANSCENDING CHALLENGES 138
MUDRA for Guidance 139
MUDRA for Facing Fear 140
MUDRA for Contentment 141
MUDRAS for Your HEALTH AND BEAUTY 142
MUDRA for Vitality and Letting Go 143
MUDRA for Protecting Your Health 144
MUDRA for Lower Spine 145
MUDRAS for LOVE 146
MUDRA for Releasing Anxiety 147
MUDRA for Opening Your Heart 148
MUDRA of Opening Your Crown 149
MUDRAS for SUCCESS 150
MUDRA for Inner Security 151
MUDRA for Self-Confidence 152
MUDRA for Diminishing Worries 153

SCORPIO 154

MUDRAS for TRANSCENDING CHALLENGES 156
MUDRA for Relaxation and Joy 157
MUDRA for Protection 158
MUDRA for Empowering Your Voice 159

MUDRAS for Your HEALTH AND BEAUTY 160
MUDRA for Overcoming Addictions 161
MUDRA for Balancing Sexual Energy 162
MUDRA for Preventing Burnout 163

MUDRAS for LOVE 164
MUDRA for Chakra Six-Truth 165
MUDRA for Trust 166
MUDRA for Powerful Speech 167

MUDRAS for SUCCESS 168
MUDRA for Calming Your Mind 169
MUDRA for Wisdom 170
MUDRA for Releasing Negativity 171

SAGITTARIUS 172

MUDRAS for TRANSCENDING CHALLENGES 174
MUDRA of Good Speech 175
MUDRA for Patience 176
MUDRA for Preventing Exhaustion 177

MUDRAS for Your HEALTH AND BEAUTY 178
MUDRA for Strong Nerves 179
MUDRA for Recharging 180
MUDRA for Preventing Burnout 181

MUDRAS for LOVE 182
MUDRA for Opening Your Heart 183
MUDRA for Facing Fear 184
MUDRA for Guidance 185

MUDRAS for SUCCESS 186
MUDRA for Rejuvenation 187
MUDRA for Prosperity 188
MUDRA for Mental Balance 189

CAPRICORN 190
MUDRAS for TRANSCENDING CHALLENGES 192
MUDRA for Opening Your Crown 193
MUDRA for Releasing Negativity 194
MUDRA for Protection 195
MUDRAS for Your HEALTH AND BEAUTY 196
MUDRA for Protecting Your Health 197
MUDRA for Anti-Aging 198
MUDRA for Strong Nerves 199
MUDRAS for LOVE 200
MUDRA of Love 201
MUDRA for Releasing Guilt 202
MUDRA for Inner Security 203
MUDRAS for SUCCESS 204
MUDRA for Relaxation and Joy 205
MUDRA for Higher Consciousness 206
MUDRA for Creativity 207

AQUARIUS 208
MUDRAS for TRANSCENDING CHALLENGES 210
MUDRA of Divine Worship 211
MUDRA for Trust 212
MUDRA for Empowering Your Voice 213
MUDRAS for Your HEALTH AND BEAUTY 214
MUDRA for Preventing Exhaustion 215
MUDRA for Uplifting Your Heart 216
MUDRA for Strong Nerves 217
MUDRAS for LOVE 218
MUDRA for Patience 219
MUDRA for Opening Your Heart 220
MUDRA of Two Hearts 221
MUDRAS for SUCCESS 222
MUDRA for Concentration 223
MUDRA for Sharp Mind 224
MUDRA for Yin and Yang 225

PISCES 226
MUDRAS for TRANSCENDING CHALLENGES 228
MUDRA of Relaxation and Joy 229
MUDRA for Overcoming Addictions 230
MUDRA for Calling the Gods of Earth 231
MUDRAS for Your HEALTH AND BEAUTY 232
MUDRA for Preventing Burnout 233
MUDRA for Healing Your Heart Chakra 234
MUDRA of Invisibility..235
MUDRAS for LOVE 236
MUDRA for Overcoming Fear 237
MUDRA for Happiness 238
MUDRA of Yin &Yang 239
MUDRAS for SUCCESS 240
MUDRA for Opening Your Crown Chakra...241
MUDRA for Concentration..242
MUDRA for Trust...243

ABOUT THE AUTHOR 245

MUDRAS for ASTROLOGICAL Signs ~ by SABRINA MESKO

The Mudra practice is a complimentary healing technique,
that offers fast and effective positive results.

Mudras work harmoniously with other traditional,
alternative and complementary healing protocols.

They help restore depleted subtle energy states
and optimize the practitioner's
overall state of wellness.

Introduction

Ever since I can remember, I have been fascinated by the never ending view of the stars in the sky and the presence of other mysterious planets. As a child I wondered for hours about where does the Universe end and when my Father explained the possibility that time and space exist in a very different way than we imagined, my mind went wild with possibilities.

I was however quite skeptical about astrology in general until one day in my early youth, a dear friend introduced me to a true Master of Vedic Astrology. He quickly and completely diminished any of my doubts about how precise certain facts can be revealed in one's Celestial map. It was as if an invisible veil had been removed, and I was granted a peek over to the other side. The astrologer also adamantly pointed out that nothing is written in stone and one's destiny has a lot of space to navigate thru. You can make the best of the situation if you know your given parameters.

My fascination and use of astrological science continues to this day and compliments and enriches my work with other observation techniques that I use when consulting.

One is born with character aspects and potential for realization of mapped-out future events, but there is always a possibility that another road may be taken. This has to do with the choices we make. Free will is given to all of us, even though often the choices we have seem to be very limited. But still, the choices are always there, forcing us to consciously participate and eventually take responsibility for our decisions, actions, and consequences..

The science of Astrology has been around for millenniums and even though some people are still doubtful, I always remind them that there is no disputing the fact, that the Moon affects the high and low tide of our Oceans - hence our bodies consisting mostly of water are affected by planetary movements in many fascinating and profound ways. Even the biggest skeptic agrees with that fact.

The Love of the Universal Power for each one of us is unconditional, everlasting and omnipresent. No matter what kind of life-journey you have, it is the very best one designed especially for you, rest assured.

And when you are experiencing life's various challenges and wishing for a smooth ride instead, keep in mind that a life filled with lessons is a life fulfilling its purpose. The tests you encounter in your daily life are your opportunities.The wisdom learned is your asset, and the experiences gained are your wealth.

Your Spirit's abundance is measured by the battles you fought and how you fought them. Did you help others and leave this world a better place in any way? Your true intention matters more than you know.

Each one of us has a very unique-one of a kind celestial map placed gently, but firmly and irrevocably into effect at the precise time of our birth. There are certain aspects of one's chart that reveal possible character tendencies and predisposed behavior in regards to love, partnerships, maintaining one's health, pursuit of success and a way of communicating.

The benefits of knowing and understanding the effects of your chart on various aspects of your life can be profound. It can help you understand and prepare ahead of time for certain circumstances that are coming your way, which increases the possibility of a better quality of life in general.

If you knew that a specific time period could be beneficial for your career wouldn't it be good to know that ahead of your plans? If you are aware that certain aspects of your physical constitution are predisposed to a weakness or sensitivity, wouldn't it be beneficial to pay attention and prevent a possible future health ailment?

If you can foresee that a certain time will be slower for you in achieving positive results, wouldn't it be wise to use that time for preparation for a more fortuitous timing? How many times have you attempted to pursue a dream of yours that just didn't seem to want to happen? And when you were completely exhausted and disillusioned, the fortunate opportunity presented itself, except now you were tired, overwhelmed and had no energy or enthusiasm left. Having such information ahead of time would offer you the chance to save your energy during quiet, less active time, so that when your luck is more likely, you can seize the opportunity and make the most of it.

Since writing my first books on Mudras a while ago, my work has expanded into many different areas, however I always included Mudras into my new ventures. When I designed International Wellness and Spa centers, I included Mudra programs to share these beneficial techniques with a wide audience. I included Mudras into my weekly TV show and guided large audiences thru practice on live shows.

Mudras will forever fascinate me and I have been humbled and excited how many practitioners from around the world have written me, grateful to have these techniques and most importantly really experiencing positive effects in time of need. Therefore it has been a natural idea for me to combine these two of my favorite topics and create a series of Mudra sets for all twelve Astrological signs.

The Mudras depicted in this book are specifically selected for each astrological sign with intention to help you maximize your gifts and soften the challenges that your celestial map contains. It is important to know that each astrological chart or shall we say celestial map, contains information that can be used beneficially and there are no "bad signs" or "better sings."

Your chart is unique as are you. By gaining information, knowledge and understanding what the placements of the planets offer you, your path to self knowledge is strengthened.

I hope this book will attract astrology readers as well as Mudra seekers and practitioners to help you utilize the beneficial combination of both these fascinating techniques. It is a unique marriage when you merge these two ancient techniques, complimenting and embellishing each other, all with a clear purpose to help you recognize your absolute highest potential.

Knowledge will help you experience the very best possible version of your life. The biggest mystery of your life is You. Discover who you are and enjoy the journey. And remember, no matter what life presents you with, don't forget to smile and keep a happy heart. With each experience gained you are spiritually wealthier for it. And that my friend, stays with you forever. The wisdom gained is eternally imprinted in your soul.

With cosmic Blessings,

Sabrina

Part One
Instructions for Practice

What are Mudras?

Mudras are movements involving only fingers, hands and arms. Mudras originated in ancient Egypt where they were practiced by high priests and priestesses in sacred rituals. Mudras can be found in every culture of the world.

We all use Mudras in our everyday life when gesturing while communicating and when holding our hands in various intuitive positions. Mudras used in yoga practice offer great benefits and have a tremendously positive overall effect on our overall state of well-being.

By connecting specific fingertips and your palms in various Mudra positions, you are directly affecting complex energy currents of your subtle energy body. As numerous energy currents run thru your brain centers, Mudras help stimulate specific areas for an overall state of emotional, physical and mental well being.

How do Mudras Work?

YOUR BODY POSTURE
During the Mudra practice sit in an upright position with a straight spine, with both your feet on the ground or in a cross legged position. Comfort is essential so that you may practice undisturbed and focus on proper practice positions.

YOUR EYES
Keep your eyes closed and gently lightly lift the gaze above the horizon.

WHERE
For achieving best results of ideal Mudra practice it is essential that you find a peaceful place, without distractions. Once your Mudra practice is established, you can practice Mudras anywhere.

WHEN
You may practice Mudras at any time. Best times for practice are first thing in the morning and at bedtime. Avoid practicing Mudras on a full stomach, and after a big meal wait for an hour before practice.

HOW LONG
Each Mudra should be practiced for at least 3 minutes at a time. Ideal practice is 3 Mudras for 3 minutes each with a follow up short 3 minutes of complete stillness, peace and meditation or reflection.

HOW OFTEN
You may practice Mudras every day. Explore various Mudras by selecting a Mudra that fits your specific needs for any given day.meaning the right and left side of your body while you are practicing a Mudra, creates an energy surge, opening up blocked nadis and increasing vital energy flow for regeneration and vitality.

Breath Control

Proper breathing is essential for optimal Mudra practice. There are two main breathing techniques that can be used with your practice.

LONG DEEP SLOW BREATH
Slowly and deeply inhale thru your nose while relaxing and expanding the area or your solar plexus and lower stomach. Exhale thru the nose slowly while gently contracting the stomach area and pulling your stomach in. Pace your breathing slowly and notice the immediate calming effects. This breathing technique is appropriate for relaxation, inducing calmness and peace.

BREATH OF FIRE
Inhale and exhale thru the nose at a much faster pace while practicing the same concept of expanding navel area and contracting with each exhalation. Unless otherwise noted Mudras are generally practiced with the long slow breath. The breath of fire has a energizing, recharging effect on body and is to be used only when so noted.

Chakras

Along our spine, starting at the base and continuing up towards the top of your head, lie subtle energy centers-vortexes-called charkas, that have a powerful effect on the overall state of your health and well being. The practice of Mudras profoundly affects the proper function of these energy centers and magnifies their power.

Our subtle energy body is highly sensitive to outside sensory stimuli of sound, aromas, visuals and outside electric currents that constantly surround us. Frequencies that permeate specific locations may attract or bother you. Perhaps you may feel eager to stay somewhere where the energy suits you and yet feel suffocated when the environment does not agree with you. We are all sensitive to energies, but some of us feel them more than others.

A positive blend of energies with another person can create a magnet-like effect, whereas another person's negative unharmonious subtle energy field subconsciously pushes you away.

By leading healthy lives and optimizing the proper function of charkas, you empower your subtle energy bodies adding strength to your physical body, mind and spirit. Destructive behavior like addictions and abuse weakens your Auric field and "leaks" your vital energy. By maintaining a healthy Aura-energy field, you can fine-tune your natural capacity for "sensing" places, situations and people that compliment your energy frequency.
In a state of "clean energy" you achieve capacity for high awareness and become your own best guide.

Chakras in the body

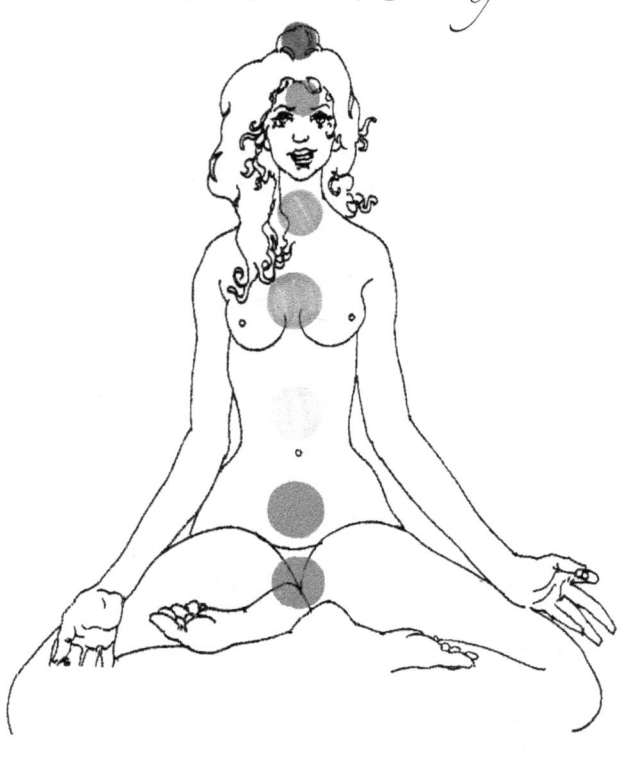

First Chakra: Foundation
LOCATION: Base of the spine
GLAND: Gonad
COLOR: Red
REPRESENTS:
Foundation, shelter, survival, courage, inner security, vitality

Second Chakra: Sexuality
LOCATION: Sex organs
GLAND: Adrenal
COLOR: Orange
REPRESENTS:
Creative expression, sexuality, procreation, family

Third Chakra: Ego
LOCATION: Solar plexus
GLAND: Pancreas
COLOR: Yellow
REPRESENTS:
Ego, intellect, emotions of fear and anger

Fourth Chakra: Love
LOCATION: Heart
GLAND: Thymus
COLOR: Green
REPRESENTS:
All matters of the heart, love, self–love, compassion and faith

Fifth Chakra: Truth
LOCATION: Throat
GLAND: Thyroid
COLOR: Blue
REPRESENTS:
Communication, truth, higher knowledge, your voice

Sixth Chakra: Intuition
LOCATION: Third Eye
GLAND: Pineal
COLOR: Indigo
REPRESENTS:
Intuition, inner vision, the Third eye

Seventh Chakra: Divine Wisdom
LOCATION: Top of the head - Crown
GLAND: Pituitary
COLOR: White and Violet
REPRESENTS:
The universal God consciousness, the heavens, unity

NADIS

Your subtle energy body contains an amazing network of electric currents called Nadis. There are 72.000 energy currents that run throughout your body from toes to the top of your head as well as your fingertips. These channels of light must be clear and vibrant with life force for your optimal health and empowerment. With regular Mudra practice you can open, clear, reactivate and re-energize your energy currents.

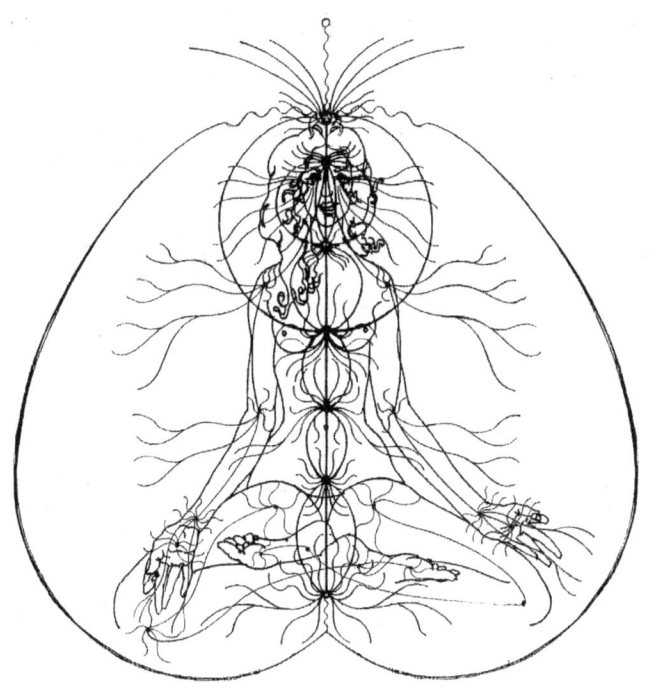

YOUR HANDS AND THE COSMOS

While practicing Mudras you are magnifying the effects of the Solar system on your physical, mental and spiritual body. Each finger is influenced by the following planets:

Thumb - God - Mars - willpower, logic, ego
Index - Jupiter - knowledge, wisdom, self confidence
Middle finger - Saturn - patience, emotional control, challenges to overcome
Ring finger - Sun - vitality, life energy, health, love
Little finger - Mercury - communication, creativity, beauty

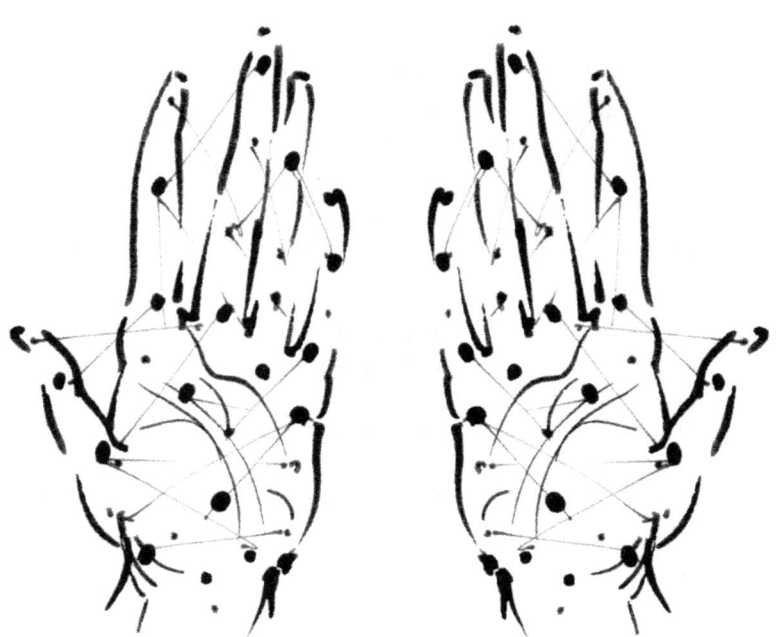

MANTRAS

Combining the Mudra practice with appropriate Mantras magnifies the beneficial effects of these ancient self-healing techniques.

The hard palate in your mouth has 58 energy meridian points that connect to and affect your entire body.

By singing, speaking or whispering Mantras, you touch these energy points in a specific order that is beneficial and has a harmonious and healing effect on your physical, mental and spiritual state.

The ancient science of Mantras helps you reactivate nadis, magnifies and empowers your energy field, improves your concentration and stills your mind.

ABOUT ASTROLOGY

The word Horoscope originates from a Latin word ORA–hour and SCOPOS–view. One could presume that Horoscope means "a look into your hour of birth". The precise moment of your birth determines your celestial set-up. An accurate astrological chart can reveal most detailed aspects of your life, your character, your gifts, your future possible events, challenges that await you, lucky events that are bestowed upon you, and your outlook for happy relationships, successful careers, accomplishments, health and many possible variations of life events. I say possible, because your decisions will determine the outcome.

There are 12 signs in the Zodiac and your birth-day reflects the position of your Sun sign. The specific positions of other planets in your chart are calculated considering the precise moment-hour and minute and of course location of your birth.

The birth time will reveal your Rising or Ascending sign, which will further determine other essential facts of your chart.

The constant transitional movements of the Planets affect each one of us differently, a time that may be difficult for some may prove supremely lucky for another and yet we are interconnected by mutual effects of continuous planetary movements. Nothing is standing still, the changes are ongoing.

On a different note, a few slow moving planets connect us in other ways, as they keep certain generations under specific aspects and influences.

We are all inseparable and in continuous motion.

There are numerous fascinating ways to use astrology and there is no doubt that the constant motion of all these powerful and majestic Planets in our Solar system affect each and every one of us differently.

Astrology can be used as an additional tool to help you continue progressing on the mysterious life journey of self discovery and self-realization.

Remember, the power of decision is yours as is the responsibility for consequences. Make peace with your doubts, pursue your dreams and relish in results.

When the outcome is less than what you expected, learn to pick yourself up and continue on, wiser with knowledge you gained, that alone being a good reason for remaining optimistic.

When the outcome surpasses your expectations, well, then you will know what to do…mostly take a breath, smile, and enjoy the moment.

YOUR SUN SIGN

There are 12 signs in the Zodiac. The day of your birth determines your Sun-sign. Most often this is the extent of average person's knowledge and interest in astrology. However, the other aspects in the astrological chart are equally as important and need to be taken into consideration. In this book your main guide is your Sun sign's dispositions, tendencies, weaknesses and gifts. Certainly there are endless combinations of charts and your Sun sign alone will not reveal the complete picture of your celestial map. For more detailed information and reflection about your chart, you need to know your ascending-rising sign.

Your Rising Sign

Your rising sign, also known as the ascendant, reflects the degree of ecliptic rising over the eastern horizon at the precise moment of your birth. It reveals the foundation of your personality. That means that even if you have the same birthday with someone else, your time of birth would create completely different aspects and influences in your chart. No two people are alike. You are one of a kind and so is everyone else. However, you may have some strong similarities and timing aspects that will be often alike. Your rising sign also reveals the basis of your chart and House placements. Your rising sign determines and is in your first house. There are 12 Houses and each depicts precise in-depth information about all aspects of your physical life, emotional make and character tendencies. It is incredibly complex and fascinating. In regards to your Mudra practice in combination with your Astrological Sign, it would be beneficial to know also your Rising sign and apply Mudras that empower your Rising sign as well. For example; if your Sun sign is Pisces, but your rising sign is Libra-it would be most beneficial to practice Mudra sets for both signs.

How to use this Book

In each book of the *Mudras for the Astrological Signs* series, you will find Mudras for different astrological signs that will help you in most important areas of your life: Health, Love, Success, and Overcoming your challenging qualities. We all have them, as we also all have gifts. You may change your Mudra practice daily as needed, and keep in mind, that certain habits or tendencies need a longer time to adjust, change, and improve. Be patient, kind, and loving towards yourself.

Mudras for Transcending Challenges

Each one of us has a few character tendencies or weaknesses that are connected to our astrological chart. To help you transcend, overcome and redirect these challenges into your beneficial assets, you can use the Mudras in this chapter.

Mudras for Health and Beauty

Each astrological sign rules certain areas of your body. The Mudras in this chapter will help you strengthen your physical weaknesses while maintaining a healthy body, and a beautiful, vibrant appearance.

Mudras for Love

The Mudras in this chapter will help you understand your love temperament, your expectations, your longings and how to attract the optimal love partner into your life. It is most beneficial to know how others perceive you in the matters of the heart. It will also help you understand your partner and their astrologically influenced love map.

Mudras for Success

The Mudras in this chapter will offer you tools to present yourself to the world in your optimal light. Often one is confused in which direction to turn or where their strength lies. Mudras will help you focus and remember your essential creative desires, help you gain self-confidence and inner security to recognize your desired and destined path. If you know what you want, and your purpose is harmonious for the better good of all, your success is within reach.

Part Two
Mudra Sets

Aries
March 21 ~ April 21

BODY
Head, eyes, brain

PLANET
Mars

COLORS
Red

ELEMENT
Fire

STONES and GEMS
Diamond, Bloodstone, Fire stone

ANIMAL
Rams and Sheep

Aries

MUDRAS FOR TRANSCENDING CHALLENGES

MUDRA for DEVELOPING MEDITATION

To sit still for a few moments is a challenge for a true Aries. You may find the thought of meditation uninteresting or uneventful. You like activity and movement and certainly most of all, you enjoy being in control. But you will be surprised how interesting, enlightening, and magical a simple short meditation can be. Your fiery power will magnify beyond measure when you make a simple effort at it. Your mind will listen to you, and you will become the pioneering leader that you desire to be. Give yourself the gift of a three minute daily Mudra meditation. Try it secretly and no one has to ever know that you - a wild and hot blooded Aries child - meditates and actually enjoys it.

Sit with a straight spine. With the four fingers of your right hand feel the pulse on your left wrist. Press lightly and feel the pulse in each fingertip. Close your eyes and concentrate on the beat of your pulse. All other thoughts are gone. With each pulse mentally repeat the mantra. Enjoy the peace and stillness of your mind in meditative state.

BREATH: Long, deep and slow.
CHAKRA: All chakras
COLOR: All colors

MANTRA: *SAT NAM*
(Truth is God's Name, One in Spirit)

MUDRA FOR TAKING YOU OUT OF DANGER

You like dangerous situations and are never afraid to cross the line. Adventures are your hobby and trouble entertains you. Even a good argument makes you feel alive and the ones who know you best are aware that you like to win the battle. That can make you appealing and attractive, but yet when you take your daring nature a step to far, better be prepared and know how to get out of trouble as quickly as you got there. This Mudra will help you balance and calm the dangerous energies that you attract and create with your daredevil nature. A great warrior knows when to quit and retrieve, so that he may exit the battle victorious and untouched. You have that gift, but on those rare occasions when you bite off more than you can chew, protect yourself with this Mudra, and create a shield of white light all around you. You may dismiss it now, but when the time comes, you'll be quick to give it a try with positive results.

Sit with a straight spine. Bend your elbows to the side and bring your arms up so that your hands are at a level of your face. Curl your fingers so that your fingertips are touching the top pads of your hands. Leave the thumb out. Hold for at least three minutes.

BREATH: Long, deep and slow.
CHAKRA : 7
COLOR: Violet

MANTRA: *GUROO GUROO WAHAY GUROO, GUROO RAAM DAS GUROO*
(As a Servant of the Infinite I receive His Wisdom)

MUDRA FOR THIRD CHAKRA

The third chakra is where we hold on to emotions like anger and fear. Many times when you hear the call of your warrior nature, you may get overpowered by the third energy center-chakra. Letting your fiery nature overwhelm you and take over is not necessary. Fire works best when contained and controlled and it is one of your life's lessons to learn to tame your fire. It is your house-your body that you reside in, so don't let the fire burn the house down. Give it some air and redirect that valuable energy into other areas of your being. This Mudra will help you spread your life force through all the chakras and prevent it from sitting in one place. Balance and tame your fire and the world will be at your feet.

Sit with a straight back. Bend your elbows and lift your hands up, elbows parallel to the ground. The palms are open facing forward, all fingers together except for the thumbs. Thumbs are pointing to the ears lightly touching your face in front of ears. Hold and keep the elbows nice and high for at least three minutes.

BREATH: Short, fast breath of fire from the navel.
CHAKRA: 3
COLOR: Yellow

MANTRA: *SAT NAM*
(Truth is God's Name, One in Spirit)

Aries

MUDRAS FOR HEALTH AND BEAUTY

MUDRA for Transcending ANGER and Preventing HEADACHE

Your sign has a tendency to be prone to head or face injuries, headache, and high fever. It is essential for your well-being, that you are familiar with this Mudra. Instead of letting the anger take over and create a headache, practice this Mudra for three minutes and let the negative energy disappear. It will tame your fiery temper under control and help you preserve your health and a cool head so that you may continue to be the "great idea person" that you are born to be.

Sit with a straight spine. Lift your hands to the level of your eyebrows. Make fists with the palms facing outward and keep the thumbs stretched pointing towards each other Press the point between your eyes and nose at the beginning of your eyebrow. Keep your eyes lightly open and direct the gaze gently towards the tip of your nose. Hold for at least three minutes.

BREATH: Long, deep and slow.
CHAKRA: All chakras
COLOR: All colors

MANTRA: *GOD AND I, I AND GOD ARE ONE*

MUDRA for Emotional BALANCE

This Mudra will help you keep balanced with your emotions which is essential for your health. Don't let your life's situations overwhelm your nervous system. Relaxation should become part of your daily routine and when you are ready to give yourself that gift, your inspirational nature will reach new levels of realization. Be a true example of a great leader that you were born to be. No emotions can sway your boat. You are calm and in harmony with the universe.

Before you practice this Mudra, drink a glass of room temperature water to balance your system. Sit with a straight spine. Place both hands with palms open under your armpits. Close your eyes, inhale and give yourself a big hug and lift the shoulders toward the ears for a few moments and then lower your shoulders, exhale, relax and open your eyes. Repeat at an easy pace for three minutes.

BREATH: Long, deep and slow.
CHAKRA: All chakras
COLOR: All colors

MANTRA: *SAT NAM*
(Truth is God's Name, One in Spirit)

MUDRA for CALMING Your MIND

Yes, you know how getting all worked up and excited isn't good for your health or a happy disposition. So when you feel tempted to explode and show your temperament, remind yourself that it will only make you fell better temporarily and that after a while you will look and feel exhausted. Because you are very expressive when displeased, everyone will see how you feel. That may not be great when you want to mesmerize someone with your charm which you have plenty off. One of great assets you can use is a calm and centered mind. That way, your power will magnify and incapacitate your opponent in an instant. But most of all, you will protect your health and preserve your youthful and glowing appearance.

Sit with a straight spine. Cross your arms in front of your chest, elbows are bend and at a ninety degree angle. Arms are parallel to the ground. Place the right palm on top of the left arm and the the top of the left hand under the right arm. All fingers are together and straight. Hold and keep the elbows nice and high.

BREATH: Long, deep and slow.
CHAKRA: 3, 4, 6
COLOR: Yellow, green, indigo

MANTRA: *OM*
(God in His Absolute State)

Aries

MUDRAS FOR LOVE

MUDRA to OPEN Your HEART

You love conquering your chosen target and will just about always do it successfully. Your hot sexual nature will take over and the object of your desire will be at your feet sooner rather than later. But you also need a lot of stimulation and unless your lover knows how to keep you guessing and chasing, you will quickly become bored. That may bring you into the habit of always chasing after someone new. You will avoid a deeper involvement and will leave before the romance has a chance to grow. But only when you allow your love to develop from the purely sexual fiery conquest into a full blown affair of the heart, will you finally experience true happiness. You will be magically transformed and mesmerized and will learn to love deeply from your heart. You need to let go, open your heart, and let yourself experience the difference, the bond and mutual dance of love and sex. At the moment of realization you will transform, evolve and become very loyal to your chosen love. Happiness on a new and deeper level will emerge.

Sit with a straight spine. Lift your hands up in front of your heart and create a cup, palms facing up. All fingers are spread apart. The palms and fingers are not touching. Keep the fingers stretched as antennas of energy and visualize your heart area opening up.

BREATH: Long, deep and slow.
CHAKRA: 4
COLOR: Green

MANTRA: *SAT NAM*
(Truth is God's Name, One in Spirit)

MUDRA for Sixth Chakra - TRUTH

Your charm, sensuality, love of danger, and adventure in your love life will have its price. To juggle all the potential activity and mesmerized conquests you need to be and are quite clever with words, which means undoubtedly many times the truth will be "adjusted". The truth will be truth no more. This habit may hurt you when the time comes and you get out of conquest mode and really fall in love. Instead of a tendency to serve yourself, you have to respect and consider the heart of your love partner. As uncomfortable as it may feel, strive to develop the habit of being truthful with your chosen one. You will be loved for who you are, all imperfections included. Telling the truth will set you free and help you truly relax at last. This newly found habit will greatly help you with your own insecure tendency to fell jealous.

Sit with a straight spine. Bend your elbows and lift your arms up so that the elbows are parallel to the ground. Palms are facing out and all fingers are together. Hold for at least three minutes. Concentrate on your Third Eye.

BREATH: Long, deep and slow.
CHAKRA: 6
COLOR: Indigo

MANTRA: *EK ONG KAR*
(One creator, God is One)

MUDRA OF TWO HEARTS

Being in love means you are in love with someone, and a very important fact is: there are two of you in the relationship. No one knows exactly what goes on in a relationship, except the two that are in it. In love you are passionate, magical, irresistible, but also bossy and impulsive. That may be a real test for your lover. Remember to consider your lover's opinion, ask about their feelings and consult with them before assuming you are on the same page. That will spare you much conflict, help you avoid an argument and replace it with harmony and love. As an exercise before making a hasty decision, just for a moment consider how your lover would feel about your plan of action. Your intuitive answer will be immediate and clear. This approach with the same final result will make them love and adore you even more-if that is at all possible, and you will be pleased with yourself that on top of the great passion you posses also great tact.

Sit with a straight spine. Connect the index and the thumb fingers forming a circle. Extend all other fingers, keeping them spread out. Lift your arms up in front of your heart. Palms are facing outward and hands are crossed over each other, left in front of right. Hook the small fingers together. All the fingers are extended. Hold for three minutes.

BREATH: Long, deep and slow.
CHAKRA: 4
COLOR: Green

MANTRA: *SAT NAM*
(Truth is God's Name, One in Spirit)

Aries

MUDRAS FOR SUCCESS

MUDRA for GUIDANCE

You are courageous and bold, driven and decisive. A great pioneer and inventor of new revolutionary projects and endeavors. You also posses a great sense of intuitive perception. In order to really take the full advantage of all these wonderful talents, you will magnify them by learning how to really listen to your inner voice of wisdom. Be still for a moment, so you can hear your guiding voice that is bubbling with new inventive ideas never before heard of, seen or experienced. When you connect with your inner guide, nothing will stop you and things will happen quickly, explosively and magically. Rely on your inner wizard and watch your ideas come to life.

Sit with a straight spine. Place your hands together in front of your chest. Little fingers are pressed together to form a cup. Palms are facing towards the sky. Leave a very small opening between the sides of the little fingers. Gently focus your eyes towards the tip of your nose towards the palms. Have a clear question. Hold for three minutes, relax, be calm and wait for a clear answer.

BREATH: Long, deep and slow into your palms.
CHAKRA: 7
COLOR: White

MUDRA FOR PATIENCE

You posses great drive, know how to fearlessly take the initiative and have a youthful excitement about your endeavors. That means that very often, after you've planted your revolutionary ideas, you expect the fruits to ripen overnight. Well, that is impossible. Some things need maturing and time for growth. This is the opportunity for you to practice patience. All in due time, every flower needs its time, every fruit needs nourishment and light. Provide that for your seed and practice patience. Before you know it, just after you realize there is no need to be in a tremendous hurry, your fruits will ripen.

Sit with a straight spine. Make circles with the tips of your middle fingers and thumbs. Keep the rest of the fingers straight. Your upper arms are parallel to the floor and elbows are out to the the sides. Your hands are at the level of your ears. Fingers are pointing towards the sky and palms are facing front. Hold for three minutes, breathe and keep the elbows nice and high.

BREATH: Long, deep and slow
CHAKRA: 6, 7
COLOR: Indigo, white

MANTRA: *EK ONG KAR SAT GURU PRASAAD*
(One creator, Illuminated by God's Grace)

MUDRA FOR EFFICIENCY

There are times when you are overcome with fiery and exciting new ideas or projects. It seems that you begin them under impossible circumstances, and against all odds. Yet they take off, and you as well as everyone else can see you are onto something big. This is when you need to pay special attention. A weakness of yours is that you quickly loose interest and before a projects is completed you are ready to move on and conquer the next impossible thing. Here are a few choices: either you surround yourself wit an amazing team of people who are going to finish the revolutionary idea that you started, or you learn to be persistent and complete your work yourself. In either case you will need to be on top of your game and very efficient. This way, no mountaintop is unreachable, nothing is unattainable, and success is yours.

Sit with a straight spine. Bend your elbows to the side and raise your hands to the level of your heart. Palms are facing your chest, a few inches away from your body. Your hands overlap and the palm of the right hand is placed over the back of the left hand. All the fingers are extended, the thumb tips are pointing towards each other. Hold the hands and forearms parallel to the ground. Practice for at least three minutes.

BREATH: Long, deep and slow.
CHAKRA: 4, 6
COLOR: Green, indigo

MANTRA: *ATMA PARMATHA GURU HARI*
(Soul, Supreme Soul, the Teacher in His Supreme Power ad Wisdom)

Taurus

April 21 ~ May 21

BODY
Throat, neck, thyroid

PLANET
Venus

COLORS
Pastel Blue, green, pink

ELEMENT
Earth

STONES and GEMS
Emerald

ANIMAL
Cattle

Taurus

MUDRAS FOR TRANSCENDING CHALLENGES

MUDRA FOR POWERFUL INSIGHT

Your determined nature is often the driving force and the reason behind your much desired success. But on every road there are circumstances that slow us down. Sometimes these unplanned stops are very necessary learning experiences. No matter how brilliant you are, there will come a time sooner or latter that you will be mistaken about something. Yet, admitting to being wrong is one of those impossible things for you that you very much dislike. It is extremely difficult for you not to claim victory. But remember, you will loose much less energy, if you wisely admit to your error and quickly move on. Yes, it is a humbling experience and no one likes it, but you can avoid this uncomfortable scenario, by carefully assessing a situation ahead of time. Practice this Mudra and it will help you recognize a possible mistake. Then, you can cleverly adjust your approach and emerge wise and victorious- your favorite outcome.

Sit with a straight back, elbows out to either side. Raise your hands until they meet above the navel point. The back of the left hand rests in the right palm and the thumbs are crossed, left over right.

BREATH: Long, deep and slow.
CHAKRA: 6
COLOR: Indigo

MUDRA for Meditation of CHANGE

You love your home and there is nothing more appealing to you than a cozy snugly evening in your plush environment. You dislike being taken away from your precious and special home. You also are not very fond of change in general, especially under rushed circumstances. But life is full of surprises and your home-bound attitude could be holding you back. It is also important to realize and accept that every good thing in life came with a change as well. Therefore it is very beneficial for you to accept, welcome, and not delay necessary change. This Mudra will help you relax, accept and sail smoothly through life's changes. Dare to be adventurous!

Sit with a straight back. Curl the fingers into fists, the fingertips pressing in the upper pads of the hands. Connect the hands of all knuckles and the pads of the thumbs. The thumbs are extended and the fingertips touching. The connected hands are held in front of the navel with thumbs directed slightly upwards towards your heart. Hold and concentrate on the energy in your hands.

BREATH: Long, deep and slow.
CHAKRA: 6, 7
COLOR: Indigo, violet

MANTRA: *ONG NAMO GURUDEV NAMO*
(I bow to the Infinite Creative Consciousness and Divine Wisdom)

MUDRA for Evoking Inner STRENGTH

Oh yes, those comfortable and luxurious days that you so adore. There is no secret about the lifestyle you seek and enjoy. But there is also a slight tendency to get too comfortable and laid back and dare we say, maybe a tiny bit lazy. Well, it happens to the best of us, but for those days when you know you just must get yourself together and snap out of that comfy zone, this Mudra will help you gather the inner power and engage in some productive activity. After all, you are in this world to accomplish something as well, and if you want to continue to enjoy that luxurious home environment, you need to get busy.

Sit with a straight back. Curl your index fingers and curl your thumbs over them. Straighten the other three fingers. Your right hand is slightly under the left hand, your middle two finger pads touching the joints of the left hand. Place your hands in front of your chest, keeping the elbows up out out the sides so that your forearms and hands make lines parallel to the ground.

BREATH: Inhale thru the nose and shape your lips into an O, and exhale with a whistle.
CHAKRA: 3, 4
COLOR: Yellow, Green

Taurus

MUDRAS FOR HEALTH AND BEAUTY

MUDRA FOR A POWERFUL VOICE

Your sign rules the voice and neck area. Thyroid is also under Taurus influence therefore it is most important to keep yourself strong and healthy in that aspect. Proper diet, exercise, and healthy lifestyle are a must. This Mudra will help you activate, recharge and enhance your communication skills, and who knows-you may even start singing beautiful arias in the shower. On a more serious note, it is most important to know how to communicate your power to the rest of the world, be it personal or professional in nature.

Sit with a straight back. Place your hands in front of your chest, palms apart and all fingertips touching. All fingers are spread apart. Inhale and press together the thumbs and the index fingers. Exhale and relax. Now inhale and press together the thumbs and the middle fingers. Exhale and relax. Continue the same way with the ring and little fingers. Practice for three minutes and finish up the cycle.

BREATH: Long, deep and slow.
CHAKRA: 5
COLOR: Blue

MUDRA FOR RECHARGING

You are very fond of creature comforts and love luxury. One of your favorite things is to get pampered and have plenty of time for rest and relaxation. It is therefore every important for your entire being that you take full advantage of any free time you have. Maybe you just have few minutes a day when you can steal away and enjoy some peace. You need a quick pick me up. This Mudra is excellent for that occasion and will help you recharge within minutes. You will feel as if you've been resting an entire afternoon. Visualize a beautiful place in nature while practicing this Mudra and replenish your body, mind and spirit.

Sit with a straight back. Extend your arms straight out in front of you, parallel to the ground.
Make a fist with your right hand. Wrap your left fingers around the fist, with the bases of the palms touching, thumbs close together and extended straight up.

BREATH: Long, deep and slow.
CHAKRA: 1, 2, 7
COLOR: Red, orange, violet

MUDRA FOR REJUVENATION

You love all things of beauty and have exquisite taste. That is one of the reasons that you love to surround yourself with beautiful people, things, art or other material belongings. Preservation of your stunning appearance is quite important to you and you are master of all things that make one beautiful. If a new product that guarantees to preserve your youthful appearance just arrived on the market, you will be the one to know about it first. You also hate being rushed and could be very comfortable lounging timelessly in a spa. This Mudra will offer you just what you need. It will instantly rejuvenate you and soothe your senses with the ocean-like hush that you create while massaging your ears. Close your eyes and imagine you are sitting at the edge of an ocean. Time and pressure don't exist. Breathe and enjoy.

Sit with a straight back. Place both palms of your hands directly on your ears. Circle your hands and massage your ears in a circular motion in the direction away from your face-counter clockwise. Listen to the sound of "*the ocean*" that you are creating with your hands.

BREATH: Long, deep and slow.
CHAKRA: 5, 6, 7
COLOR: Blue, indigo, violet

MANTRA: *OM*
(God in His Absolute State)

Taurus

MUDRAS FOR LOVE

MUDRA for Higher CONSCIOUSNESS

While you are a lover that knows how to experience romance in true sense of the word, create a dream romantic fantasy environment, and mesmerize your partner, you also posses the capacity to quickly loose your temper. All the romance flies out the window instantly. It is therefore very important, to be able to elevate and extract yourself from the situation that is upsetting you, and employ your higher awareness to help you see what is the real reason for disharmony. It may be your overprotective character that is limiting the freedom your loved one needs to feel. Before you let your temper get the best of you, distance yourself from the situation for a few minutes and practice this Mudra. Within moments you will see a possible other aspect to the situation and find a harmonious solution.

Sit with a straight back. Put your palms together and extend your elbows to either side. Lift your hands in front of your heart, fingers pointed away from you. Each thumb is on the fleshy mound below the little finger of the same hand. Put the palms together with the right thumb snugly above the left thumb. The bottoms of the hands touch firmly. Hold the hands a few inches away from the body.

BREATH: Long, deep and slow.
CHAKRA: 3, 7
COLOR: Blue, violet

MANTRA: *OM*
(God in His Absolute State)

MUDRA OF TRUTH

Your tendency to be secretive can work both ways. You may be able to create an amazing surprise, keep the deep secrets of your best friend, and never let anyone know about it. Or you may keep some secrets from your loved one. Sometimes is a real relief to finally let the truth be revealed and just be yourself. Being able to confide in your lover will bring you closer and tighter. Leaving them out may create an unwanted distance. You need to be courageous to tell the truth and that is not always the easiest thing in the world. This Mudra will help you feel confident and find the best approach to speak out, be honest and truthful, and release a deep secret. Chances are it will help your lover do the same which will deepen your bond. Give it a try.

Sit with a straight back. Bend your elbows and lift your arms up so that the elbows are parallel to the ground. Palms are facing out and all fingers are together. Hold for three minutes.

BREATH: Long, deep and slow.
CHAKRA: 6
COLOR: Violet

MANTRA: *EK ONG KAR*
(One Creator, God is One)

MUDRA FOR TRUST

Trust is the fundamental strength in every relationship. But first you must trust yourself. The ultimate trust is the trust in the creative Universal energy that is a part of every and each one of us. Trust that everything happens at the right time, that there is an amazing individual plan for every one of us, and trust that you will meet the love of your life when you least expect it. Your stubborn nature sometimes argues with this trust and wants things it's way. Release this tendency or at least soften it up a bit, so that you may be able to enjoy life's surprises including the most delicious one of falling in love and meeting your match. If the person does not fit your fixed idea of the "perfect one", take a deep breath, relax and trust. You will be surprised. It turns out, someone knows you better than you know yourself.

Sit with a straight back. Make a circle with your arms arched up over your head, palms down. Put the right palm on top of the left. Lightly press the thumb tips together, keep your back straight and visualize a circle of white protective light around you.

BREATH: Short, fast, breath of fire focusing on the navel.
Practice for a minute and relax with deep slow breath for another two minutes.
CHAKRA: 7
COLOR: Violet

MANTRA: *HAR HAR HAR WAHE GURU*
(God's Creation, His Supreme power and Wisdom)

Taurus

MUDRAS FOR SUCCESS

MUDRA FOR A SHARP MIND

In order to pursue a successful life, you need to develop a very necessary quality of a sharp and quick mind. Knowing what you want and how to make your way towards your goal is essential. When you forget about exercising the mind like a fine musical instrument, you forget how powerful you really are. It is all in the mind. You tend to lead others with your business expertise. Take your natural tendency to a higher level and guide your determined nature so that you won't waste precious energy. While you are very ambitious, it is wise to reflect on all your options before going forward full force. Take a moment for yourself, breathe, relax and focus your mind with this Mudra.

Sit with a straight back. Hold the left hand up as though to clap, then with the index and middle fingers of the right hand slowly and with strong pressure walk up the center of the left palm to the very tips of the middle and ring fingers. Walk up as you inhale and down as you exhale.

BREATH: Long, deep and slow.
CHAKRA: 5, 6
COLOR: Blue, indigo

MANTRA: *HARA HARE HARI*
(The Creator in Action)

MUDRA for Releasing Negative Emotions

No matter what the circumstances are and how right you may be, it is never wise to loose temper in a business environment. Your stubborn nature may push you into a corner that may prove challenging to get out of. Don't ignore the danger of drowning just because you won't admit the water is too deep. When you are bursting with negative emotions, find a quite place where you can have a few moments alone and release the negativity. You will emerge more powerful and focused.
To loose temper means to loose control over yourself. That is something that will never reflect strength in any way. Center yourself and collect the inner power that will allow you to become the powerhouse you were born to become. This Mudra will help you along.

Sit with a straight back. Bend your arms and make fists with both hands. Bring them up in front of your heart. Cross the hands over each other, palms turned outwards. Hold the Mudra across the chest with the left arm on the outer side.

BREATH: Long, deep and slow.
CHAKRA: 4
COLOR: Green

MUDRA for Inner INTEGRITY

Knowing yourself and your good as well as weaker habits is empowering. Being able to admit that you are wrong may be difficult, but the longer you delay that realization, the more painful the ending. It shows great strength of character and self esteem when you recognize and admit your error.
Every successful person failed many times before succeeding and certainly we've all been wrong at times. We improve and learn from past mistakes. So take a deep breath and empower yourself with the truth. By admitting your weaknesses like the love of extreme comfort and maybe a trace of laziness, you are making a great first step towards change, but only if you make that choice.
Stay true to your heart and pure ideas, and your success will manifest, rest assured.

Sit with a straight back. Bend your elbows and lift your upper arms parallel to the ground. Bring your hands to ear level, palms facing out. Curl the fingers inward and point the thumbs out toward your ears. Hold for three minutes and relax.

BREATH: Short, fast, breath of fire from the navel.
CHAKRA: 4
COLOR: Green

Gemini
May 22 ~ June 21

BODY
Shoulders, lungs, arms
nervous system

PLANET
Mercury

COLORS
Yellow, orange

ELEMENT
Air

STONES and GEMS
Agate

ANIMAL
Small bird, butterfly, monkey

Gemini

MUDRAS FOR TRANSCENDING CHALLENGES

MUDRA FOR CONTENTMENT

There are two people inside of you and that offers more gifts and benefits, but also creates some inner friction. You are "talented for two" and therefore the inner dialogue needs more attention and discipline. If you ignore this aspects, you will experience some kind of inexplicable discontent when everything is wonderful, and often a wavering of moods for no reason. Understanding yourself and this aspect is most important, and yet, balancing your powerful inner energies requires more work and time. This Mudra is very beneficial for taming these aspects and should be practiced daily. Then, your two "Inner artists" will live in peace and everlasting harmony.

Sit with a straight back and lift your hands in front of your stomach area. Connect your thumb and the middle finger of the right hand and the thumb and the little finger of the left hand. Relax the rest of the fingers and hold your hands a few inches apart, palms up. Hold for three minutes, the make fists with both hands and relax.

BREATH: Long, deep and slow.
CHAKRA: 3
COLOR: Yellow

MANTRA: *SARE SA SA SARE SA SA SARE HARE HAR*
(God Is Infinite in His Creativity)

MUDRA for RELAXATION and JOY

Your restless spirit and creative ideas are alive and active in every moment of your day. Taking a real relaxing vacation with no other purposeful activity does not appeal to you. Being the social butterfly that you are, you often miss the perfect opportunity to relax and just be-a very necessary and vital part of creative process. Once you allow yourself to take a breather and look at the ocean or the sunset, your mood is instantly uplifted, your ideas soar and you are renewed and truly happy. This Mudra will help you accomplish that, even when you do not have the luxury of an amazing environment. Just close your eyes and transport yourself wherever your heart desires, but be still, breathe and experience the true meaning of relaxation.

Sit with a straight back, lift up your hands up in front of your chest. Make a fist with your left hand, tucking the thumb inside. Wrap the right hand around the left and place your right thumb over the base of the left thumb. Concentrate on your third Eye area and hold for three minutes. Later, extend your practice to eleven minutes.

BREATH: Long, deep and slow.
CHAKRA: 3, 4
COLOR: Yellow, green

MANTRA: *HAREE HAR HAREE HAR*
(God in His Creative Aspect)

MUDRA for PROTECTION

With your generous and happy heart you may often forget to practice any caution. You may just trust that this world is perfect, pure, and everyone is harmless. Become more aware of other people's mindset, motivations and tendencies to take advantage of anyone who allows it. It does not mean looking at everyone and everything with suspicion, it only means to be aware, and do not give away the last thing you have just because someone asks you too. Learn to look out for yourself with discipline and caution. To protect yourself from any negative people, situations or circumstances, practice this Mudra, stay calm and focused. This world is an adventure, but it is also a jungle that needs to be walked thru with caution.

Sit with a straight spine. Cross your left hand over your right one and place them on your upper chest. Palms are facing you and all fingers are together. Hold for three minutes and feel the immediate energy shift.

BREATH: Long, deep and slow.
CHAKRA: All chakras
COLOR: All colors

MANTRA: *OM*
(God Is His Absolute State)

Gemini

MUDRAS FOR HEALTH AND BEAUTY

MUDRA for Uplifting Your HEART

Sensitive that you are, you need to take care of your heart, so that your feelings and emotions do not take you into dark waters of gloom. Then it seems like your other twin sowed up-and we don't really want him/her do we? By being aware that you are extra sensory gifted and at the same time delicate, you need to take good care of your body-instrument and protect your gifts. Pleasant, calm environment and people are a must and no emotional stress should be allowed for too long. Often life takes us into directions we never expected, and tests us precisely in areas of our weakness, thus your prompt awareness is of great importance. Guard your inner peace and heart each and every day.

Sit with a straight back, and lift up your arms shoulder level, elbows bent and parallel to the ground. Tuck your thumbs under your armpits and keep the rest of your fingers straight and together. Your hands should be above your breasts, palms facing down. As you inhale, the distance between the middle fingertips gets bigger; as you exhale, the middle fingertips should touch or cross each other. With each inhalation feel the healing energy expand your heart and chest area. Continue for three minutes and relax.

BREATH: Long, deep and slow.
CHAKRA: 4
COLOR: Green

MUDRA for Diminishing WORRIES

You are very youthful and adaptable and may give an appearance of lightheartedness and a carefree disposition, but deep inside, you tend to worry and are quite restless. This of course is not constructive, productive or healthy. Learn to do your best and then truly let go and let Universe work to your benefit. This Mudra will help you release the worry habit and establish a state of calm inner peace, so that you can visualize and attract positive outcomes, developments and people into your life.

Sit with a straight back. Bring your hands in front of your chest with the palms facing up. The sides of the little fingers and inner sides of the palms are touching. Now bring the middle fingertips together, perpendicular to the palms. Extend the thumbs away from the palm. Hold and keep the fingers stretched as little antennas for energy.

BREATH: Long, deep and slow
CHAKRA: 4, 5, 6
COLOR: Green, blue, indigo

MUDRA for Healthy Breast and HEART

Your vulnerable areas of heart, lungs, respiration and chest area require your care and attention. That encompasses all levels of special care: physical, mental and emotional. Releasing challenging emotions associated with matters of heart and positive mental dispositions in relation to these aspects as well. Extra physical care is required to assure long lasting health of this region, breathing exercise in the open are ideal. Regular practice of this Mudra will help you keep your chest area clear of dense negative energy, and continuously recharged with new vital life force.

Sit with a straight back. Relax your arms at your sides with the palms facing forward. Then alternatively bend each elbow so that the forearms come toward the heart center as rapidly as possible. When your right hand is at your chest, the left hand is away from the body and when the left hand is at your chest, the right hand is away from the body. Do not bend the wrists or hands and do not touch the chest. Continue at a rapid pace four times while you inhale, four times while you exhale, until you feel hot, then relax for a few minutes.

BREATH: Long, deep and slow.
CHAKRA: 4
COLOR: Green

Gemini

MUDRAS FOR LOVE

MUDRA OF TWO HEARTS

You are quite the lively, witty romantic, and it may be very clear in your mind and heart who the love of your life is, but your other "invisible twin" may give out different signals all together. Appearing non-committal in matters of the heart will create some understandable frustration and heartache for your partner. That is why it is ever important for you to expand your thinking, communication habits, perception, and awaken your awareness of your partner and the consequences of your perhaps tackless actions. Your lover needs assurance that your temporary doubts have nothing to do with them, but your inner restlessness. To help you achieve and maintain harmony in love, practice this Mudra and focus on aligning your energy and needs with that of your lover. The temporary "hick-up" will pass and all will be well again in your land of love.

Sit with a straight spine. Connect the thumbs and index fingers on each hand and spread out and extend all other fingers. Lift your arms in front of your heart, cross arms in front of you - left in front of right, palms facing out and little fingers hooked onto each other. Keep fingers nice and extended thru the practice.

BREATH: Long, deep and slow.
CHAKRA : 4
COLOR: Green

MANTRA: *SAT NAM*
(Truth Is God's Name, One in Spirit)

MUDRA for HEALING Your HEART Chakra

You are very charming and desirable, but there will be times when like the rest of us, you will need to learn a few love lessons. For example; how forgetting your lovers birthday is a bad idea, or how shyness doesn't always pay off, and how sometimes taking responsibility for your actions or words is the best way to resolve an unnecessary conflict. On the other hand, you may need to heal your heart when hurt by someone who simply does not understand your sensitive nature. It is most important that you learn how to strengthen and protect your heart and navigate thru the love and romance process with some confidence and lightness. Your perfect mate will appear when the time is perfect. And that is not up to you, so just breathe, relax, and keep your heart harmonious and loving, always open to new adventures.

Sit with a straight spine. Lift your right hand up, elbow bent, your hand at the level of your face. Make a fist and leave only the index finger extended, pointing up. Place your left hand on your chest above your breast, elbow parallel to the ground. Hold and feel the energy shifting in your body. Keep the elbows nice and high.

BREATH: Long, deep and slow
CHAKRA : 4
COLOR: Green

MUDRA for Right SPEECH

Some people prefer very demonstrative and open verbal communication of love and affection. This is where you may run into some challenges-a light, harmless joke may be misunderstood, a simple expression of fear of commitment may send your lover into a state of distress. Some of us are more sensitive than others, and while you are sensitive yourself, you are less cautious with what you express. Not to worry, just pay a tiny bit more attention when talking about the matters of the heart- your lover hangs on every word and it will really brighten their day, if you gift them with a romantic expression and gesture, tell a few sweet words, and make them feel they are in heaven- after all, you are a very romantic partner who needs and loves being a team. Tell them so.

Sit with a straight spine. Relax your arms, keep your elbows at your sides, and bring your hands up in front of your stomach, palms open and flat, facing up. Spread your fingers gently and touch the tips of the ring fingers together, the right little finger is under the left little finger. Now concentrate and tense the thumb and the index fingers without moving the fingers. Hold for a few seconds and release. Now tense the thumb and the middle fingers, again without moving. Hold for a few seconds and release. Next tense the thumb and the ring fingers. Hold and release. Lastly, tense the thumb and little fingers, hold for a few seconds and relax. Repeat the cycle reversing the little fingers.

BREATH: Long, deep and slow.
CHAKRA : 3, 5
COLOR: Yellow, blue

MANTRA: *HAR DHAM HAR HAR*
(God is the Creator)

Gemini

MUDRAS FOR SUCCESS

MUDRA for SELF - CONFIDENCE

There is a real genius inside of you and many are aware if it, but this world still requires for you to come out of your creative space and confidently express who you are. Your inner wavering and indecisive nature may present an obstacle when you are on your way to the top. This demands some inner work on your part. Establishing a strong sense of confidence before exposing yourself to the world, where there will be praise but also naturally criticism-this requires a strong confident persona. You can have all that and more, but work at it. Do not dismiss this detail, for it is the total of all elements that creates success, genius alone won't do. After all, this is planet Earth and you can't be in the clouds all the time. Stand strong and confident on the ground and your will be rewarded.

Sit with a straight back. Lift your hands up to the level of your solar plexus with elbows bent to the sides. Bend the middle, ring, and little fingers and touch them back to back. Extend the index fingers and thumbs and press them together. The thumbs are pointed toward you and the index fingers away from you.

BREATH: Long, deep and slow
CHAKRA: 3, 6
COLOR: Yellow, indigo

MANTRA: *EK ONG KAR SAT GURU PRASAD, SAT GURU PRASAD EK ONG KAR*
(The Creator Is the One That Dispels Darkness and Illuminates Us by His Grace)

MUDRA for Powerful INSIGHT

As a versatile intellectual and eloquent individual it is understandably challenging when outside demands start interfering with your pure creative spirit. But the mastery of success requires your capacity to be adaptable and manage to find that fine-tuned balance between what brings you joy and what also works for your to finally enjoy the fruits of your labor. Everyone has to adapt a bit, to better convey their message. Do not take this personally, take it as a necessary element of the process. This Mudra will help you find that perfect combination and blend the magical elements that can be fine-tuned and finally presented in such a fashion that it will absolutely work. Take your time and reflect, it is as important as all other steps on this journey.

Sit with a straight back, elbows out to either side. Raise your hands until they meet above the navel point. The back of the left hand rests in the right palm and the thumbs are crossed, left over right.

BREATH: Long, deep and slow.
CHAKRA : 6
COLOR: Indigo

MANTRA: *SAT NAM*
(Truth is God's Name, One in Spirit)

MUDRA FOR SHARP MIND

When time for action is here, you need to be equipped to act quickly, decisively and confidently. That is not always the easiest challenge. Any kind of wavering can cost you a golden opportunity. In moments like this, take your time and practice this Mudra to achieve a state of a sharp mind where the ideas are clear as a whistle and the final picture is set in your mind. Once you have achieved that state, there will be no stopping you and you will be heard, seen and paid attention too. Much earned success will arrive!

Sit with a straight spine. Hold the left hand up in front of you chest as if ready to clap, then with an extended index and middle finger of your right hand firmly walk up the center of the left palm, starting at the bottom of the palm and continuing to the very tips of middle and ring fingers of the left hand. Walk up and down your palm while maintaining pressure.

BREATH: Long, deep and slow.
CHAKRA: 3, 6
COLOR: Yellow, Indigo

MANTRA: *HARA HARE HARI*
(The Creator in Action)

MUDRAS for CANCER

Cancer

June 22 ~ July 22

BODY
Chest, breasts

PLANET
Moon

COLORS
Silver, gray

ELEMENT
Water

STONES and GEMS
Pearl

ANIMAL
Creatures with shell

Cancer

MUDRAS FOR TRANSCENDING CHALLENGES

MUDRA FOR INNER SECURITY

You are emotionally very sensitive and loving. That is an endearing quality and gives you the capacity for compassion for all living creatures and special sense of protection for your close family. But that aspect can cause you to emotionally swing the other way and be over touchy and perhaps even moody. You need to empower your emotional inner security and stability and this Mudra will help you achieve just that.

Sit with a straight back, place your hands in reversed prayer pose, hands touching back to back at the level of your heart and solar plexus. Hold the pose for one and a half minutes, then repeat with the palms pressed together in a prayer pose.

BREATH: Long, deep and slow.
CHAKRA: 3, 4
COLOR: Yellow, green

MANTRA: *AD SHAKTI AD SHAKTI*
(I Bow to the Creator's Power)

MUDRA for SELF - CONFIDENCE

When emotions run deep your entire physical body and your mind are affected. This may cause you feeling less secure and confident thus propelling your cautious nature even deeper into that direction. Your strong and vivid imagination plays a role as well and it is very important to balance your self confidence and stability as a part of your daily routine. This Mudra will help you establish a firm and confident disposition which will work wonderfully with your other lovely qualities.

Sit with a straight back. Lift your hands up to the level of your solar plexus with elbows bent to the sides. Bend the middle, ring, and little fingers and touch them back to back. Extend the index fingers and thumbs and press them together. The thumbs are pointed toward you and the index fingers away from you.

BREATH: Long, deep and slow.
CHAKRA: 3, 6
COLOR: Yellow, indigo

MANTRA: *EK ONG KAR SAT GURU PRASAD, SAT GURU PRASAD EK ONG KAR*
(The Creator Is the One That Dispels Darkness and Illuminates Us by His Grace)

MUDRA for Diminishing WORRIES

Your great love and deep caring nature for your family brings along also some worry and unrest. Very often you will find yourself in a situation to be taking care of your entire extended family and overseeing and guiding everyone thru their life journeys. Naturally an element of clinginess could be present, and it is important to learn to let the birds fly out of the nest as well. They will always return to you for advice, that will never change. But endless worrying won't do, therefore this Mudra will help you overcome that tendency, so that you too can breathe, and enjoy life.

Sit with a straight back. Bring your hands in front of your chest with the palms facing up. The sides of the little fingers and inner sides of the palms are touching. Now bring the middle fingertips together, perpendicular to the palms. Extend the thumbs away from the palm. Hold and keep the fingers stretched as little antennas for energy.

BREATH: Long, deep and slow
CHAKRA: 4, 5, 6
COLOR: Green, blue, indigo

Cancer

MUDRAS FOR HEALTH AND BEAUTY

MUDRA for Emotional BALANCE

Your gifts and intuitive powers require a clear calm instrument in order to operate at maximum capacity. Emotions need to be in perfect balance in order for you to be able to tune-in and sense proper decisions, future events and opportunities. In the area of your health it is essential that you protect yourself from unnecessary emotional stress and everything that it brings along. This Mudra will work wonders for your overall emotional state and comfort. With regular practice you will be able to magnify your intuition while preserving your health.

Before you practice this Mudra, drink a glass of room temperature water to balance your system. Sit with a straight spine. Place both hands with palms open under your armpits. Close your eyes, inhale and give yourself a big hug and lift the shoulders toward the ears for a few moments and then lower your shoulders, exhale, relax and open your eyes. Repeat at an easy pace for three minutes.

BREATH: Long, deep and slow.
CHAKRA: All
COLOR: All

MANTRA: *SAT NAM*
(Truth is God's Name, One in Spirit)

MUDRA FOR STRONG NERVES

Your rich emotions and sympathetic nature will often get you into situations of fighting for others, weaker than yourself while protecting them from harm. This requires a certain level of energy and perseverance that wears on your nervous system. In order to maintain a healthy physical state in that area, you need to pay special attention to protecting and preserving your nervous system. This Mudra offers you great help with this aspect and requires regular practice, in completely peaceful environment, and with focused attention. Do not forget to be as concerned about your welfare as you are for that of others. You can only help them if you remain strong and healthy yourself- in body, mind and spirit.

Sit with a straight spine. Lift your left hand at ear level, palm facing out. Connect the thumb and middle finger and stretch out other fingers. Place your right hand in front of the solar plexus, palm facing up. The thumb and little finger are touching while other fingers are straight. **This position is reversed for men.**

BREATH: Long, deep and slow.
CHAKRA: 3, 4
COLOR: Yellow, green

MUDRA for Removing DEPRESSION

By knowing you are vulnerable and prone to emotional mood swings, you can prepare and prevent this occurrence from happening. Proper diet is essential as is sufficient rest and relaxation. If you ignore these vulnerable aspects you could unnecessarily suffer from depression, which would require more work and discipline to overcome. Therefore it is most beneficial, that you establish heathy habits and proper care for yourself in every aspect-with a healthy lifestyle and environment.

Sit with a straight spine. Stretch your arms in front of you, hands up at heart level. Put the backs of your hands together, with your fingers pointing away from your body, making sure that as many as possible knuckles touch. Your forearms are as parallel to the ground as possible, thumbs pointing down to the ground. This Mudra creates a great deal of tension on the back part of your hands, but do not practice too long if your muscles are straining.

BREATH: Long, deep and slow.
CHAKRA: 4, 5, 6
COLOR: Green, blue, indigo

MANTRA: *HARI NAM SAT NAM SAT NAM HARI NAM*
(God is Truth in Creation)

Cancer

MUDRAS FOR LOVE

MUDRA FOR RELEASING GUILT

You are a wonderful and caring partner, reliable and filled with pure love. You create ever new romantic situations and are eager to care for children and family. Sometimes you may become overly sentimental about the past and struggle to move on as life inevitably does. The old days were romantic, but so can be today. With this strong tendency to hang on to the past, you may carry along some unnecessary feelings of guild and take on your shoulders more responsibility than appropriate. This Mudra will help you prevent that from happening and help you enjoy your love life without unnecessary self inflicted burdens.

Sit with a straight back, elbows out to the sides, and bring your palms up to the level between your stomach and heart center. Palms are facing up toward the sky, right hand resting in left. Upper arms are slightly away from the body. Breathe slowly and deeply.

BREATH: Long, deep and slow.
CHAKRA : 3
COLOR: Yellow

MANTRA: *I AM THINE WAHE GURU*
(I am Thine, Divine Teacher within)

MUDRA FOR HAPPINESS

Being in the here and now and enjoying every second of it-that is the key. After you have taken care of everything and everybody, be present with your lover and enjoy the supremely blissful romantic environment you helped create. This is what love is all about. Toss the worry, nothing else matters. This Mudra will help you learn how to enjoy these moments of profound happiness that will forever imprint in your spirit, mind and heart, and carry you thru thick and thin. Thats what pure love is- everlasting and forever.

Sit with a straight spine. Bend your elbows and bring your arms to your sides, away from your body. Elbows are just below the level of the shoulders. Palms are facing forward. Stretch the index and middle fingers and bend the ring and little fingers, pressing them into the palms firmly with the thumbs. Hold for three minutes and relax.

BREATH: Long, deep and slow.
CHAKRA: 4
COLOR: Green

MANTRA: *SAT NAM*
(Truth is God's Name, One in Spirit)

MUDRA for PREVENTING STRESS

Often stress is something we create out of unnecessary habits or situations. When various challenging dynamics present themselves to you, you have a choice. What is truly important and worth your time and effort? You can not protect every single vulnerable human being or living creature, so be selective to make an impact and reserve the rest of your energy for yourself and your loved ones. You are a delicate instrument and for optimal health stress needs to be eliminated as much as possible. Make time for loving home environment that will heal and empower you.

Sit with a straight spine. Bend your elbows and bring your forearms in front of your solar plexus area parallel to the ground. Rest the back of the left hand in the palm of the right hand, both palms facing up. Fingers are straight and together. Hold for three minutes and concentrate on your breath.

BREATH: Long, deep and slow.
CHAKRA: 3
COLOR: Yellow

Cancer

MUDRAS FOR SUCCESS

MUDRA FOR PROSPERITY

You have an excellent sense for business and can be extremely shrewd. The financial matters are important to you and you take security very seriously. Thru it all, fulfillment is more important to you than pure ambition and when you find your joy in your work, you like stability and continuity. This Mudra will help you establish and attract a prosperous mental disposition and environment to secure the stable life that you need and desire.

Sit with a straight back. Bring your hands in front of you, fingers together and palms facing down. Press the sides of the index fingers together and hold for a second. Now flip your hands over o that the palms are facing up toward the sky for a second and the edges of the little fingers are touching. Keep repeating and chant the mantra HAR with each change of hand position. Continue the practice for eleven minutes and rest.

BREATH: Short, fast breath of fire from the point of the navel, repeated with each mantra and Mudra movement.
CHAKRA: 1, 2, 3
COLOR: Red, orange, yellow

MANTRA: *HAR HAR* (God, God)

MUDRA FOR A CALM MIND

When you are closing that major business deal and can taste the sweet flavor of success, it is most important that the emotions do not get the best of you and suddenly expose you as a vulnerable, overly sensitive creature that you are. Keeping a calm mind becomes a priority and with that accomplished you can master any situation anytime, anyplace. This Mudra will help you maintain a serene and peaceful state of mind and can be practiced even during a business meeting.

Sit with a straight spine. Cross your arms in front of your chest, elbows bent at a ninety-degree angle and arms parallel to the ground. The right hand is on top of the left arm and left hand below the right arm. All fingers are together and straight. Hold and keep the arms from sinking for three minutes then relax and be still.

BREATH: Long, deep and slow.
CHAKRA: 3, 4, 6
COLOR: Yellow, green, Indigo

MANTRA: *OM*
(God in His Absolute State)

MUDRA for MENTAL BALANCE

We all know that emotional and mental states are closely interconnected-in your case even more so. That presents a possible situation of your emotions taking over even when it may be to your disadvantage. Be in charge and a master of your emotions-this way your mind will be able to work to it's fullest and greatest potential. Let your mental brilliance have an opportunity to shine. To assure that you are prepared and take advantage for every professional golden opportunity, practice this Mudra and maintain optimal mental clarity and unwavering balance. Success is assured.

Sit with a straight spine. Place your hands at solar plexus level in front of you and interlace the fingers backward with palms facing up. Fingers are pointing up and the thumbs are straight.

BREATH: Long, deep and slow.
CHAKRA: All
COLOR: All

MANTRA: *GOBINDAY, MUKUNDAY, UDAARAY, APAARAY, HARYNG, KARYNG, NIRNAMAY, AKAMAY*
(Sustainer, Liberator, Enlightener, Infinite, Destroyer, Creator, Nameless, Desireless)

Leo

July 23 ~ August 23

BODY
Heart, spine, back

PLANET
Sun

COLORS
all colors of the sun

ELEMENT
Fire

STONES and GEMS
Gold, Ruby

ANIMAL
Cats

Leo

MUDRAS FOR TRANSCENDING CHALLENGES

MUDRA for Receiving God's Law

You are strong, powerful and as the "King of the Jungle" you have a hint of a bossy streak. Your opinions are heard and your enthusiastic, warm-hearted nature is present in everything you touch. But when you are such a self-assured leader, sometimes the responsibility that comes along with the territory can cramp your free creative spirit. It is a good time to remember that there is a higher power than yourself, that actually plays the larger, decisive role in everyone's life. Remaining open to that Universal power and understanding that your gifted artistic nature is a direct result of God's generosity, it is wise to consciously reconnect with it, and show humble respect while continuously increasing your receptivity and wealth of talents.

Sit with a straight back. Lift the right hand to heart level, palm facing down, and the left hand to your solar plexus area, palm facing up towards the sky. Leave enough space between the palms for a small ball. Elbows are to the side. All fingers are together and straight. Hold the Mudra and concentrate on the energy between your palms.

BREATH: Long, deep and slow.
CHAKRA: 7
COLOR: Violet

MANTRA: *OM*
(God in His Absolute State)

MUDRA for Readjusting Your PERCEPTION

You are generous and loving in nature, however you dislike interference or disobedience in regards to your opinions or rules. And yet, the best leaders know their people and the land, and are capable of seeing the world from many points of view. This Mudra will help strengthen this capacity in you, so that you may be able to adjust and improve your leading tendencies while truly understanding the needs and situations of others. This way, others will trust your guiding powers even more, and together you can create a powerful and harmonious empire.

Sit with a straight back. Make circles with the thumbs and index fingers and spread out the rest of the fingers. Lift your arms so your elbows are perpendicular to the ground and your hands are at eye level. Now move your hands toward each other until you can look through the openings of your fingers. As you separate your hands, take a long, slow inhale. As you bring them together in front of your face, exhale, long, deep, and slow. Observe the change of perception with the movement of your hands.

BREATH: Long inhale when hands apart, long exhale when moving hands together.

CHAKRA: 6, 7
COLOR: Indigo, violet

MANTRA: *SA TA NA MA*

(Infinity, Birth, Death, Rebirth)

MUDRA FOR INNER INTEGRITY

For all the power and capacity to be the center of the Universe, it is interesting that after all, you are very sensitive and can be easily hurt. This will often involve your pride, which is healthy in small portions and under certain circumstances, but do not let it come in your way of reaching your goal. You can stay true to yourself and be happily fulfilled. How to keep that inner integrity and maintain a balance with everything you are doing? Practice this Mudra to find that inner balance and empower the capacity to clearly sense what feels and is the right thing to do or say in any circumstance. With power comes responsibility- wear it well and you will impress all, including yourself.

Sit with a straight back. Bend your elbows and lift your upper arms parallel to the ground. Bring your hands to ear level, palms facing out. Curl the fingers inward and point the thumbs out toward your ears. Hold for three minutes and relax.

BREATH: Short, fast, breath of fire from the navel.
CHAKRA: 4
COLOR: Green

Leo

MUDRAS FOR HEALTH AND BEAUTY

MUDRA for Healthy BREAST and HEART

Taking care of your heart is essential and that means in all aspects and areas. A healthy diet, and physical activity to keep the stamina is important. However, your enthusiasm can sometimes prevent you from remembering where your limitations are. You do need to rest and take a break and no matter how fiery your creative spell is, take a breather so you can return invigorated and recharged. This Mudra is excellent for keeping your heart and breast healthy and filled with fresh vital energy, working at optimal capacity.

Sit with a straight back. Relax your arms at your sides with the palms facing forward. Then alternatively bend each elbow so that the forearms come toward the heart center as rapidly as possible. When your right hand is at your chest, the left hand is away from the body and when the left hand is at your chest, the right hand is away from the body. Do not bend the wrists or hands and do not touch the chest. Practice at a rapid pace four times while you inhale, four times while you exhale, until you feel hot, then relax for a few minutes.

BREATH: Long, deep and slow with motions as described.
CHAKRA: 4
COLOR: Green

MUDRA for Activating Lower CHAKRAS

Your back and spine need attention and proper care. A healthy spine affects your entire mental and emotional disposition, as well as the level of physical strength and endurance. With regular exercise and care, it can be the pillar of your strength and overall health. For a strong and recharged base and lower spine, practice this Mudra and help keep it clear of stuck energy, always recharged and healthy.

Sit with a straight back. Place both hands at waist level, thumbs open with palms facing down. All fingers are stretched and together, the tips of the middle fingers an inch apart. As you inhale, concentrate on expanding the lower area of your stomach. When you exhale, contract the stomach and bring your fingertips closer until they almost touch. Concentrate on bringing vital creative energy into that area of your body, filling it with life force.

BREATH: Start slowly and after a minute increase the tempo into the breath of fire, after a minute slow down and return to the slow, deep breath.
CHAKRA: 1, 2
COLOR: Red, orange

MANTRA: *SAT NAM*
(Truth is God's name, One in Spirit)

MUDRA FOR MIDDLE SPINE

Keeping your heart healthy reflects also in care for you middle spine-your center of power. Proper breathing is your essential tool for maintaining optimal balance and harmony in that region. Make it a regular habit and dedicate every day a few minutes of your time to this Mudra practice. Truly focus with your mind on recharging and revitalizing your center. This way, your creative ideas will have a proper chance to come to fruition, so you can be happy, fulfilled and can share your inspiring loving nature with others.

Sit with and place your fists on your knees or in front of you with elbows bent. Leave the thumbs pointing up. Concentrate on your thumbs, sending healing energy to the middle area of your back. Keep the thumbs stretched and hold for three minutes.

BREATH: Long, deep and slow.
CHAKRA: 3, 4
COLOR: Yellow, Green

MANTRA: *OM*
(God in His Absolute State)

Leo

MUDRAS FOR LOVE

MUDRA for Opening Your HEART

Everyone loves a strong and self-assured partner, but make sure that your strength does not develop into an overly domineering disposition. It is perfectly fine to be vulnerable and it is also very acceptable that you are not always right about everything you say or do. Strength also comes in acceptance of one's weakness and not let pride prevent you from enjoying a healthy and fulfilling love relationship. And yet, with your other side of extreme and quick sensitivity, it is a good idea to take a few minutes, get centered and truly open your heart to your lover. Juts relax and be, no need to be the unbeatable leader every second of the day. Let your lover feel an equal partner and play fair. It will be much more fun.

Sit with a straight spine and lift your hands in front of your heart with palms and fingers open as if creating a cup. Keep all the fingers stretched and feel healing energy pouring into your fingertips and the area of your heart.

BREATH: Long, deep and slow.
CHAKRA: 4
COLOR: Green

MANTRA: *SAT NAM*
(Truth is God's Name, One in Spirit)

MUDRA for COMPASSION

You are quite the idealist in love aspects and sometimes that can be an impossibly demanding role for your partner. Nobody is perfect and when you suddenly realize that is a fact, be gentle and kind. Expand your heart in compassion and truly make an effort to understand your lover. Give them some air and let them find their own voice or individualism. And then a magical thing will happen- you will fall in love with them even more - perhaps again idealizing them in a different context. In either case, expanding your capacity to love unconditionally by accepting one as they are, will alleviate your unreasonable disappointment and you will experience profound love on a whole different level, perhaps even better.

Sit with a straight spine. Extend your arms out to the sides parallel to the ground with the palms turned front. Stretch out the fingers and hold them still. Turn your head to the right side and back to the center four times, then to the left side and back to the center four times. Continue for a few minutes and concentrate on your heart center. Become aware of the energy in your palms.

BREATH: Inhale long once as you move your head to the right, and exhale long once you move your head back to center. Repeat four times to each side. Relax and sit still for a few minutes.

CHAKRA: 4
COLOR: Green

MANTRA: *AKAL AKAL SIRI AKAL*
(Timeless Is the One Who Achieves Perfection of the Spirit)

MUDRA for Uplifting Your HEART

Being overly sensitive is a weakness that does not bring you much joy. Sulking over an unimportant detail, event or spoken word, is best released and forgotten. Concentrate on the happy aspects and allow your naturally sunny disposition to shine thru the unnecessary clouds of your temporary gloomy mood. When you are in need to overcome this tendency, practice this Mudra and instantly uplift your heart and general outlook. Sunny days filled with love lay ahead. Your partner will be overjoyed to have you back.

Sit with a straight back, and lift up your arms shoulder level, elbows bent and parallel to the ground. Tuck your thumbs under your armpits and keep the rest of your fingers straight and together. Your hands should be above your breasts, palms facing down. As you inhale, the distance between the middle fingertips gets bigger; as you exhale, the middle fingertips should touch or cross each other. With each inhalation feel the healing energy expand your heart and chest area. Continue for three minutes and relax.

BREATH: Long, deep and slow.
CHAKRA: 4
COLOR: Green

Leo

MUDRAS FOR SUCCESS

MUDRA FOR MENTAL BALANCE

When you have a clear vision of your mission, nothing will stand in your way. However, more often than not, in order to realize your dream, you have to work with others and need to compromise a bit. This can present an obstacle and be very frustrating for you. Keep the eye on the ball and with some give and take you will achieve your goal. The world is full of compromises and this is one of them. In order to be able to accomplish that without too much stress, take some time and practice this Mudra to achieve absolute mental calm and focus. Clearly select a happy middle route to keep everyone happy and still arrive where you want to. Be tactful and play the game to win. Later, your compromises will become smaller and when you succeed on a large scale, everything may be done your way.

Sit with a straight spine. Place your hands at solar plexus level in front of you and interlace the fingers backward with palms facing up. Fingers are pointing up and the thumbs are straight.

BREATH: Long, deep and slow.
CHAKRA: All
COLOR: All

MANTRA: *GOBINDAY, MUKUNDAY, UDAARAY, APAARAY, HARYNG, KARYNG, NIRNAMAY, AKAMAY*
(Sustainer, Liberator, Enlightener, Infinite, Destroyer, Creator, Nameless, Desireless)

MUDRA FOR POWERFUL INSIGHT

You are highly creative and love being in constant and ongoing project mode. Centre stage is right at home for you and you will easily acquire an enthusiastic and loyal audience. Organizing a large scale event or place of business is something you can tackle since you have a tremendous capacity for seeing the big picture. Your eyes are set on the highest prize and you make that clear. However, you motivation is the creative process and not pure ambition. The key to your achieving all and more than you ever desired, is to be be able to take some time and reassess the proper steps to get there. This may require you letting another person take over some aspects that they do better. Be open to equal collaborators and show flexibility. This will become your asset and make you unstoppable and undefeated. The best leaders are superbly clever with their warriors, they do not do everything themselves. Carefully select your "army" and watch your dreams become a reality.

Sit with a straight back, elbows out to either side. Raise your hands until they meet above the navel point. The back of the left hand rests in the right palm and the thumbs are crossed, left over right.

BREATH: Long, deep and slow.
CHAKRA: 6
COLOR: Indigo

MUDRA for Better COMMUNICATION

You know what you want and there is no doubt about it. However, some people may not be as capable, savvy and fast in following your direction. This is the time you can become bossy, patronizing and intolerant. It does not make the process easier, it only creates tension and unnecessary conflict. Stay focused, calm, and truly concentrate on remaining a good, pleasant, kind and respectful communicator. You are very loving and will attract loving people into your life that may feel hurt when you fail in proper communication with them. You can do anything you set your mind to, so this is one of those things- become a role model in diplomatic and harmonious communication and see the positive results manifest.

Sit with a straight spine. Connect the index and thumb fingers, creating a circle. Stretch out the rest of the fingers and rest your hands, palms facing down on your thighs or elevated in front of you. Hold for three minutes, breathe and relax.

BREATH: Long, deep and slow.
CHAKRA: 1, 2
COLOR: Red, orange

MANTRA: *RAA MAA*
(I Am in Balance Between the Sun and the Moon, the Earth and the Ether)

Virgo

August 24 ~ September 22

BODY
Nervous system, stomach, intestines

PLANET
Mercury

COLORS
Navy blue, dark brown, green

ELEMENT
Earth

STONES and GEMS
Sardonyx

ANIMAL
Domestic pets, dogs

Virgo

MUDRAS FOR TRANSCENDING CHALLENGES

MUDRA for COMPASSION

Your great gift for details and your meticulous, reliable nature also creates a very high level of expectations. In other words-you are the ultimate perfectionist. You demand the best of yourself and others. Well, the reality is that sometimes these high expectations just can not be met. Your overly critical streak can take over and no one is happy, including you. To avoid succumbing to this characteristic, take a moment and truly "loosen up" the grip. See yourself in the position of the other person and open your heart to compassion and understanding. Nobody is perfect in this wold. The sooner you realize and accept that, the better for you and your level of contentment.

Sit with a straight spine. Extend your arms out to the sides parallel to the ground with the palms turned front. Stretch out the fingers and hold them still. Turn your head to the right side and back to the center four times, then to the left side and back to the center four times. Continue for a few minutes and concentrate on your heart center. Become aware of the energy in your palms.

BREATH: Inhale long once as you move your head to the right and exhale long once as you move your head back to center. Repeat four times to each side. Relax and sit still for a few minutes.

CHAKRA: 4
COLOR: Green

MANTRA: *AKAL AKAL SIRI AKAL*
(Timeless Is the One Who Achieves Perfection of the Spirit)

MUDRA for RELEASING Negativity

Your intelligence, keen observation and analytical talents are true gifts that can bring you much success. However, it is possible that when not applied properly you could be seen as overly fussy and perhaps even harsh in your assessments. In order to deliver the information in the best possible format and successfully rely the message without a trace of negativity, this Mudra will be very helpful. Practice it before meetings or important exchanges so that your true gifts are recognized and not misunderstood, or met in a defensive manner. Transform your criticism into gentle but precise "redirecting" advice.

Sit with a straight back. Bend your arms and make fists with both hands. Bring them up in front of your heart. Cross the hands over each other, palms turned outwards. Hold the Mudra across the chest with the left arm on the outer side.

BREATH: Long, deep and slow.
CHAKRA: 4
COLOR: Green

MUDRA FOR RELAXATION AND JOY

After each successfully accomplished and completed project there needs to be a time of rest and relaxation. Enjoy the fruits of your labor and breathe. Of course it would be truly exceptional, if you were able to enjoy the entire process as well, for that is the point of life. Enjoying every step of the way and not just worrying about the end result or the final outcome. Every minute and day counts, so do not delay and practice this Mudra to help you remember how to live in the moment and feel carefree, joyful and happy each and every day.

Sit with a straight back, lift up your hands up in front of your chest. Make a fist with your left hand, tucking the thumb inside. Wrap the right hand around the left and place your right thumb over the base of the left thumb. Concentrate on your third Eye area and hold for three minutes. Later, extend your practice to eleven minutes.

BREATH: Long, deep and slow.
CHAKRA: 3, 4
COLOR: Yellow, green

MANTRA: *HAREE HAR HAREE HAR*
(God in His Creative Aspect)

Virgo

MUDRAS FOR HEALTH AND BEAUTY

MUDRA FOR SECOND CHAKRA

Your vulnerable area of stomach demands special attention and care. Every occasion that requires your extra strength and energy can show consequences and strain in that region. Pay close attention and find the ideal diet for you, always creating a peaceful environment when eating. This Mudra will help you soothe, energize and protect that region so that you will overcome "nervous stomach" with ease and little effort.

Sit with a straight back. Place your left hand with palm facing down in front of your stomach area. Hold your right hand open, away from your body, the palm facing up.

BREATH: Long, deep and slow.
CHAKRA: 2
COLOR: Orange

MANTRA: *SAT NAM*
(Truth Is God's Name, One in Spirit)

MUDRA for STRONG NERVES

Your diligent and perfectionistic nature requires much patience and stamina. Your nervous system is put to a test and needs extra help and attention. That requires proper rest, a healthy diet, plenty of sleep, fresh air and generous time spend in nature. An overall holistic lifestyle and relaxation techniques are required. Mudras are ideal for you and it is most beneficial that you implement this practice into your daily life and make it a part of your required routine. This Mudra will help you maintain, preserve and protect your nerves. When you find yourself in any kind of stressful situations, take a few minutes to practice and feel immediate relief.

Sit with a straight spine. Lift your left hand at ear level, palm facing out. Connect the thumb and middle finger and stretch out other fingers. Place your right hand in front of the solar plexus, palm facing up. The thumb and little finger are touching while other fingers are straight. **This position is reversed for men.**

BREATH: Long, deep and slow.
CHAKRA: 3, 4
COLOR: Yellow, green

MUDRA FOR RELEASING ANXIETY

All that worry and your fussy, analytical nature keeps you in a continuous state of suspense, expectation and under pressure. When things sway a bit into an unknown direction, your anxiety level rises and makes everything even more intense. With your many talents and abilities you are always automatically exposed to criticism and you being your own worst judge, this is not a recipe for peace and fun. However, help is on its way! This Mudra is extremely powerful and can transform you in a matter of minutes into a serene and energetically empowered person that you want and deserve to be. Now you can be on your way and see your goals accomplished. Practice this Mudra every morning when a stressful day lies ahead and enjoy the beneficial, long lasting results.

Sit with a straight spine. Bend your elbows and raise your arms so your upper arms are parallel to the ground and extended out to the sides. Your hands are at the level of your ears, fingers spread wide and pointing to the sky. Start rotating your hands back and forth pivoting at the wrists. Practice for three minutes and be persistent. You will go thru a period when it seems difficult, but when you overcome that moment, the practice will be easy.

BREATH: Long, deep and slow.
CHAKRA: 4, 5, 6
COLOR: Green, blue, indigo, violet

MANTRA: *HARKANAM SAT NAM*
(God's Name Is Truth)

Virgo

MUDRAS FOR LOVE

MUDRA FOR OPENING YOUR HEART

You are very demanding of yourself and entertain a harsh inner monologue. In order to attract a loving partner your way, who appreciates and generously unconditionally loves you, you need to love yourself truly unconditionally as well. That means when you see things about yourself that are not so perfect, make a decision to manage and overcome that tendency, and love yourself for who you are. This Mudra will help you open your heart and allow loving energy, people and situations to come your way. You can finally relax and be happy with who you are.

Sit with a straight spine and lift your hands in front of your heart with palms and fingers open as if creating a cup. Keep all the fingers stretched and feel healing energy pouring into your fingertips and the area of your heart.

BREATH: Long, deep and slow.
CHAKRA: 4
COLOR: Green

MANTRA: *SAT NAM*
(Truth is God's Name, One in Spirit)

MUDRA FOR LOVE

Once you fall in love, the main focus should be to truly enjoy the blissful times, and soak in every minute of happiness. You will do anything and everything for your partner, but you may forget to stop worrying or nagging about your imaginary imperfections. Your partner can not continuously assure you that you are great just the way you are, you need to truly embrace yourself and let go of any self-analyzing habit. Love is peace, harmony, togetherness, and calm soothing energy no matter where you are together. Just being you in enough. Practice this Mudra and consciously absorb the essence of love in every possible way.

Sit with a straight spine and raise your hands to the either side of your head. Curl the middle and ring fingers into your palm and extend the thumbs, index fingers, and little fingers. Keep your elbows from sinking and hold for three minutes.

BREATH: Inhale for eight short inhalation counts, and exhale with one strong, long exhale.
CHAKRA: 4
COLOR: Green

MANTRA: *SAT NAM WAHE GURU*
(God is Truth, His Is the Supreme Power and Wisdom)

MUDRA FOR GUIDANCE

When you fall in love and open your heart to your lover, it is important to let go and truly let your mind have a rest. Not everything needs to be decided with your amazing mind. Matters of the heart need a different approach. You may not find it logical-the person whom you fall in love with-or even expected. Your dream partner may be completely different than you imagined or thought it would be best. This is how love is; inexplicable and unpredictable. When you mind is trying to interfere with those wonderful moments of love, you need to practice this Mudra. It will help you learn how to hear your heart and engage in heartfelt guidance. Listen and just receive, no thinking required, just absolute stillness and receptivity. Give it a try. You will be amazed and transformed.

Sit with a straight spine. Place your hands together in front of your chest. Little fingers are pressed together to form a cup. Palms are facing towards the sky. Leave a very small opening between the sides of the little fingers. Gently focus your eyes towards the tip of your nose towards the palms. Have a clear question. Hold for three minutes, relax, be calm and wait for a clear answer.

BREATH: Long, deep and slow into your palms.
CHAKRA: 7
COLOR: White

Virgo

MUDRAS FOR SUCCESS

MUDRA for SELF - CONFIDENCE

Perfectionist that you are, your expectations of yourself are super high and unrealistic. This can be partially good because you will strive to be better and will be quite disciplined about your goals. But the other side of the coin is, that you may be to harsh on yourself. When you realize that your "norm" can not be met, you may have some confidence issues to fight with. They key is to relax these demands a bit and you will see that your very best is darn close to perfect anyway. To help you strengthen your confidence, practice this Mudra with dedication and intent. Redirect your mind patterns into a positive loving inner dialogue and affirmations. You are great just the way you are.

Sit with a straight back. Lift your hands up to the level of your solar plexus with elbows bent to the sides. Bend the middle, ring, and little fingers and touch them back to back. Extend the index fingers and thumbs and press them together. The thumbs are pointed toward you and the index fingers away from you.

BREATH: Long, deep and slow.
CHAKRA: 3, 6
COLOR: Yellow, indigo

MANTRA: *EK ONG KAR SAT GURU PRASAD, SAT GURU PRASAD EK ONG KAR*
(The Creator Is the One That Dispels Darkness and Illuminates Us by His Grace)

MUDRA for CREATIVITY

When you amazing gifts of intelligence, practicality and perfectionism join, the results are achieved. The one element that needs to be implemented even more to truly produce a fulfilling new successful venture is your creativity. You need to tap into your core creative source and let your imagination fly. This Mudra will help you open up those channels and stimulate your creative energy so that what the project you work on truly surpasses everyone's imagination.

Sit with a straight spine. Connect the thumbs and index fingers, keeping the rest of the fingers straight. Bend your elbows and lift your hands to your sides with palms facing up at a sixty-degree angle to your body. Concentrate on your Third eye and meditate for at least three minutes.

BREATH: Short, fast, breath of fire from the navel.
CHAKRA: 6, 7
COLOR: Indigo, violet

MANTRA: *GA DA*
(God)

MUDRA for POWERFUL INSIGHT

Small details matter, but they are not most important all the time. Deciding what takes priority is needed to get the projects accomplished while seeing the big picture. Overworking a smaller issue takes you away from the main path. The hard worker that you are, it is essential that you make clear boundaries and are selective. Taking a moment and reflecting on priorities and dividing your workload is essential. This Mudra will help you come to a decision in this area and will assure that you have a healthy, but reasonable work tempo. Save your work energy for things that matter and are essential.

Sit with a straight back, elbows out to either side. Raise your hands until they meet above the navel point. The back of the left hand rests in the right palm and the thumbs are crossed, left over right.

BREATH: Long, deep and slow.
CHAKRA: 6
COLOR: Indigo

Libra

September 23 ~ October 23

BODY
Kidneys

PLANET
venus

COLORS
pale blue, pink, green

ELEMENT
Air

STONES and GEMS
Sapphire, Jade

ANIMAL
Small reptiles

Libra

MUDRAS FOR TRANSCENDING CHALLENGES

MUDRA FOR GUIDANCE

Being the symbol of balance you have an uncanny capacity to weight the options. When someone asks for help and advice, you will lay out all the facts and help them see the picture clearly. That is a very special gift, yet when it comes to you it may prove a bit more challenging. Weighing your options too long can turn into indecisiveness and making yourself vulnerable to distracting outside influences. You will need this Mudra to help guide you thru your hesitation and indecisive moments.

Sit with a straight spine. Place your hands together in front of your chest. Little fingers are pressed together to form a cup. Palms are facing towards the sky. Leave a very small opening between the sides of the little fingers. Gently focus your eyes towards the tip of your nose towards the palms. Have a clear question. Hold for three minutes, relax, be calm and wait for a clear answer.

BREATH: Long, deep and slow into your palms.
CHAKRA: 7
COLOR: White

MUDRA FOR FACING FEAR

You do not like being left alone and a very social. People enjoy your company and you are quite popular. However, when it comes to revolutionary causes or putting up a fight, you prefer the diplomatic route and will prefer to play it safe and won't insist on a confrontation. You enjoy peace and will always feel a duty to help preserve that. To help you overcome challenging moments of unavoidable conflict, practice this Mudra and remain untouchable and calm.

Sit with a straight back. Bend your right elbow and lift the arm up to the level of your face. Face your palm outward, as if taking a vow. Bring your left arm in front of your navel, palm facing up. Concentrate on energy being received into your palms and hold for at least three minutes. Relax and be still.

BREATH: Long, deep and slow.
CHAKRA: 3, 7
COLOR: Yellow, violet

MANTRA: *NIRBHAO NIRVAIR AKAAL MORT*
(Fearless, Without Enemy, Immortal Personified God)

MUDRA FOR CONTENTMENT

In order to get what you want, you need to know what you want in the first place. If you do not address the order of things this way, you will feel discontent and often jealous of others. Knowing yourself is the key element to achieve happiness on all levels and in all areas of your life. If you do not actively participate in the decision making process and would rather stay on the fence instead of commit to a side, it would be most beneficial if you would be able to make peace within yourself with the consequences. Take responsibility for your indecisiveness and remain content with the outcome. This Mudra will help you achieve that.

Sit with a straight back and lift your hands in front of your stomach area. Connect the thumb and middle finger of the right hand and the thumb and the little finger of the left hand. Relax the rest of the fingers and hold your hands a few inches apart, palms up. Hold for three minutes, then make fists with both hands and relax. Position is reversed for men.

BREATH: Long, deep and slow.
CHAKRA: 7
COLOR: Violet

MANTRA: *SARE SA SA SARE SA SA SARE HARE HAR*
(God Is Infinite in His Creativity)

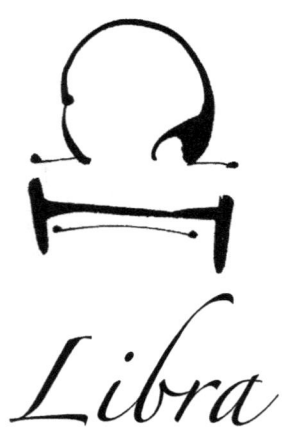

Libra

MUDRAS FOR HEALTH AND BEAUTY

MUDRA FOR VITALITY AND LETTING GO

When you feel yourself unnecessary dwelling on a certain event or circumstance, you need to " live and let go". Decision has been made and there is no need to carry unnecessary negative emotions with you. Regular exercise is important for your health as well as a healthy diet. Your sign rules the kidneys, so keeping toxins to a minimum is imperative. That includes mental and emotional restlessness. Retain your vital energy and use it for positive, harmonious and happy frame of mind. For best results practice this Mudra regularly.

Sit with a straight back and place your fists in front of you, palms facing up. Concentrate on your base chakra. Sit tall and attempt to stretch as if trying to get taller. Be aware of the ground underneath you and the life force of the earth.

BREATH: Long, deep and slow.
CHAKRA: 1, 2
COLOR: Red, orange

MANTRA: *SAT NAM*
(Truth is God's Name, One in Spirit)

MUDRA for Protecting Your HEALTH

You like a comfortable and easy going pace in life. What is important for you to remember is the need for a healthy diet, so do not let your sweet tooth get the best of you. Inactivity could cause you to gain some extra pounds that you don't need, keeping active and productive will help you keep that under control. In matters of general health pay attention to what really best suits you and do not be too gullible or easily influenced to go in the wrong direction. The best option is for you to keep an all around healthy lifestyle and take some time to find that perfect balance for yourself. After all, balance is your speciality.

Sit with a straight back. Bend your right elbow and lift your left hand up, palm facing out. The index and middle fingers are pointing up; the rest are curled with the thumb over them. Hold your left hand in the same Mudra with the two stretched fingers touching your heart. Hold for three minutes.

BREATH: Inhale for ten counts, hold the breath for ten counts, and exhale for ten counts. Pace yourself comfortably, relax and be still.

CHAKRA: All color
COLOR: All color

MANTRA: *OM*
(God in His Absolute State)

MUDRA FOR LOWER SPINE

Your sign rules the kidneys and lower back therefore it is wise to pay extra attention to these areas and keep them as healthy and vital as possible. Be disciplined and remember that preserving your health is the best investment ever made-make that extra effort and keep a wise diet and conflict free living environment at work and especially at home. You need harmony in every possible way. Practice this Mudra to help you strengthen your vulnerable areas and prevent a potential challenging situation. Harmonize your life, begin with the base-your spine. Make this Mudra a part of your morning routine.

Sit with a straight spine and make fists with both hands. Leave the thumbs stretched out and hold the hands in front of you. The palms are facing the ground and the thumbs are directed toward each other. Keep the fists strong and feel the energy pulsating in your palms. After three minutes relax your hands and rest.

BREATH: Long, deep and slow.
CHAKRA: 1, 2
COLOR: Red, orange

MANTRA: *OM*
(God in His Absolute State)

Libra

MUDRAS FOR LOVE

MUDRA for Releasing ANXIETY

Falling in love is a blessing that happens when destiny calls. You really do not have to make a decision there, for it is made for you. However, once in love, eventually decisions to move forward will have to be made and this will be a challenge for you. You are very harmonious with your partner and there will never be any arguing, except when you need extra proof that they love you unconditionally. Then you may test them, which is of course very unproductive. Instead, practice this Mudra and release our inner anxiety, wether it has to do with getting engaged, married or simply moving in together. Give it a go and you'll see, a new harmonious environment will be established and you will be even happier than before.

Sit with a straight spine. Bend your elbows and raise your arms so your upper arms are parallel to the ground and extended out to the sides. Your hands are at the level of your ears, fingers spread wide and pointing to the sky. Start rotating your hands back and forth pivoting at the wrists. Practice for three minutes and be persistent. You will go thru a period when it seems difficult, but when you overcome that moment, the practice will be easy.

BREATH: Long, deep and slow.
CHAKRA: 4, 5, 6
COLOR: Green, blue, indigo, violet

MANTRA: *HARKANAM SAT NAM*
(God's Name Is Truth)

MUDRA for OPENING Your HEART

You are a great romantic and will have no trouble mesmerizing your partner with that perfect environment you created. You may only have to fight within yourself first to get to that point. Sitting on the fence about making the first move won't pay off. So get your courage together and take a chance. This Mudra will help you open your heart to this new love, so you will recognize and experience the true meaning of unconditional. It means; no conditions, no negotiations, and not indecisiveness. Here you are, now jump.

Sit with a straight spine and lift your hands in front of your heart with palms and fingers open as if creating a cup. Keep all the fingers stretched and feel healing energy pouring into your fingertips and the area of your heart.

BREATH: Long, deep and slow.
CHAKRA: 4
COLOR: Green

MANTRA: *SAT NAM*
(Truth is God's Name, One in Spirit)

MUDRA FOR OPENING YOUR CROWN

Finding your life partner is very important to you. You may be very successful, engaged in much socializing, and surrounded by many friends. Yet, until your true love appears you will feel lonely. Being alone is something you dislike and avoid at all costs. In order to attract the right partner into your life, you need to be receptive to the Universal energy. By opening your connection to the ultimate source, you will find yourself drawn to a place and time where the perfect partner awaits. It could be around the corner or on another continent. It does not matter, what is important is that you do not resist your destiny. This Mudra will help you open your receptive sensory capacity and follow the magical path.

Sit with a straight spine. Lift your hands above your head, all fingers kept apart as if you were holding a crown on your head. Keep the arms at this level and fingers stretched the entire practice. Visualize a stream of bright white light pouring into the crown of your head and filling your entire body with healing light.

BREATH: Long, deep and slow.
CHAKRA: 7
COLOR: VIOLET

MANTRA: *OM*
(God in His Absolute State)

Libra

MUDRAS FOR SUCCESS

MUDRA FOR INNER SECURITY

Your natural God given beauty is something that you rely on. You may work in fashion, beauty, design and love luxury and all that it offers. If for a moment you feel a bit unsure about that aspect, an insecurity could spoil the best of times for you. Develop and rely on your other qualities that you are gifted with; your charming, romantic, easy going nature that is very attractive and appealing. This Mudra will help you dispel those clouds of insecurity so that you will remain the sunshine of the crowd.

Sit with a straight back, place your hands in reversed prayer pose: hands touching back to back at the level of your heart and solar plexus. Hold the pose for one and a half minutes, then repeat with the palms pressed together in a prayer pose.

BREATH: Long, deep and slow.
CHAKRA: 3, 4
COLOR: Yellow, green

MANTRA: *AD SHAKTI AD SHAKTI*
(I Bow to the Creator's Power)

MUDRA FOR SELF - CONFIDENCE

When during discussions you are not clearly voicing your opinion, it may appear that you are not secure within yourself. The truth may be that you just want to avoid taking sides, since you dislike any kind of confrontation or conflict. To help you overcome this trait which will not always serve in your best interest, practice this Mudra. It will help you participate in discussion with confidence as your opinion does matter and is valuable. Engage your strong diplomatic talents and achieve peace within the group. Be confident that you can do that, for it is your hidden talent and gift.

Sit with a straight back. Lift your hands up to the level of your solar plexus with elbows bent to the sides. Bend the middle, ring, and little fingers and touch them back to back. Extend the index fingers and thumbs and press them together. The thumbs are pointed toward you and the index fingers away from you.

BREATH: Long, deep and slow.
CHAKRA: 3, 6
COLOR: Yellow, indigo

MANTRA: *EK ONG KAR SAT GURU PRASAD, SAT GURU PRASAD EK ONG KAR*
(The Creator Is the One That Dispels Darkness and Illuminates Us by Hs Grace)

MUDRA for Diminishing WORRIES

Since you like luxury and a comfortable life, you need to make plenty of money to make it all happen. This creates of course a certain level of pressure for pursuing and maintaining the lifestyle that comes with a high price. However, a top executive job presents a certain level of loneliness which you won't like. Perhaps it would be best to find a happy medium and compromise. So you may have to sacrifice a few fancy perks, but it will help you sleep peacefully at night. Make a good plan of your wants, needs and sacrifices, then it will be easier for you to find that golden balance. When worry overcomes you, practice this Mudra and remember that every problem has a solution. It is all within your reach.

Sit with a straight back. Bring your hands in front of your chest with the palms facing up. The sides of the little fingers and inner sides of the palms are touching. Now bring the middle fingertips together, perpendicular to the palms. Extend the thumbs away from the palms. Hold and keep the fingers stretched as little antennas for energy.

BREATH: Long, deep and slow.
CHAKRA: 4, 5, 6
COLOR: Green, blue, indigo

MUDRAS for SCORPIO

Scorpio
October 24 ~ November 22

BODY
Sexual organs

PLANET
Pluto

COLORS
Dark red, maroon

ELEMENT
Water

STONES and GEMS
Opal

ANIMAL
Insects

Scorpio

MUDRAS FOR TRANSCENDING CHALLENGES

MUDRA FOR RELAXATION AND JOY

Your intense and competitive nature pushes you into overdrive. Your deep, complex, and analyzing mind needs down time filled with peace and solitude. Make it a point to schedule regular relaxation times for yourself where you can rejuvenate and refresh, so that you are ready and enthusiastic to return to your projects with renewed energy. This Mudra is an excellent tool for you to let go and learn to spend some easy and peaceful time with yourself.

Sit with a straight back, lift up your hands up in front of your chest. Make a fist with your left hand, tucking the thumb inside. Wrap the right hand around the left and place your right thumb over the base of the left thumb. Concentrate on your third Eye area and hold for three minutes. With time, extend your practice to eleven minutes.

BREATH: Long, deep and slow.
CHAKRA: 3, 4
COLOR: Yellow, green

MANTRA: *HAREE HAR HAREE HAR*
(God in His Creative Aspect)

MUDRA FOR PROTECTION

You are secretive and get fascinated by the darker side of this world. You feel you can play with fire and nothing will ever happen to you. Invincible and indestructible. Often your curiosity will get the best of you and you may find yourself caught or even trapped in a dangerous place or habit. Call upon the Divine power to protect and guide you at all times. Practice this Mudra and consciously select a wiser path. Life can be just as adventurous without careless danger.

Sit with a straight spine. Cross your left hand over your right one and place them on your upper chest. Palms are facing you and all fingers are together. Hold for three minutes and feel the immediate energy shift.

BREATH: Long, deep and slow.
CHAKRA: All
COLOR: All

MANTRA: *OM*
(God in His Absolute State)

MUDRA FOR EMPOWERING YOUR VOICE

Just like the scorpion can sting with an unexpected bite, so can you with your sharp words. Fearless in conflict or confrontations, your sarcastic capacity can wound a more sensitive and delicate person. Transcending your power into a state of higher awareness and guiding your counterpart towards a spiritual realization will bring you more happiness, inner fulfillment, and better karma. Practice this Mudra when you are tempted to "sting", and overcome this hurtful urge. Your natural magnetism will charm your opponent and disarm them completely.

Sit with a straight back, bend your elbows and lift them parallel to the ground, while you lift your hands in front of you at the level of your throat. Turn the right palm outward and the left palm towards you. Bend your fingers and hook your palms together, while pulling them apart. Keep your shoulders down while applying pressure to the pull.

BREATH: Long deep and slow.
CHAKRA: 5
COLOR: Blue

Scorpio

MUDRAS FOR HEALTH AND BEAUTY

MUDRA for Overcoming ADDICTIONS

Your fascination with the darker underworld sometimes seduces you into a self destructive pattern. You may think you are invincible for a while, but do not let careless experiments get the best of you. Your physical body has a certain stamina, but overindulgence is a trait you must overcome with focus and intention. We learn from all our experiences and so will you. Your sign has the amazing capacity to rise from the ashes of a burning, destructive fire, and experience a true rebirth. Next time, you are hopefully older and wiser. Practice this Mudra when you feel the pull of the darker side and truly prove yourself that you are stronger than your temptations.

Sit with a straight back. Make fists with both hands and then extend the thumbs out. Press the thumbs on the temples where you feel a slight depression. Clench your teeth, lock the back molars, and keep your lips closed. Vibrate the jaw muscles by alternating the pressure on the molars. A muscle will move in rhythm under the thumbs. Feel it massage the thumbs as you continue to apply firm pressure with them. Concentrate on your Third eye area as you do this. Continue for three to eleven minutes. Now relax your arms and place them at your sides, with the thumbs and index fingers forming a circle. Hold and relax.

BREATH: Long, deep and slow.
CHAKRA: 1, 2, 3, 4, 5
COLOR: Red, orange, yellow, green, blue

MUDRA for Balancing SEXUAL Energy

Your sign rules sex organs and you are most likely a deeply sensual and sexual being. However, you do know that anything in excess can attract disharmony. Therefore it is wise that you take extra precaution and learn to balance your drive so that you are the one in charge. Keep in mind that simply following your desires does not guarantee happiness and after you fixate on your conquest, take a moment and truly reflect if this pursuit is worth it. If it is just a compulsive habit, take a step back and go deeper within yourself. The fulfillment you so desire requires a multi-layered satisfaction. And remember, every time you physically merge with someone, you blend the energy fields of the two and carry this specific frequency with you for quite a while. So be selective and protective. This Mudra will help you redirect your sexual nature to a healthy place.

Sit with a straight back, elbows slightly out to the side. Clasp your hands together, interlocking your fingers. Leave the left little finger outside of the hand. By placing the right thumb on top of the left thumb we empower our masculine side, and when the left thumb is placed on top of the right thumb we recharge the feminine side of our nature. Press your hands together in this Mudra, hold for three minutes and relax.

BREATH: Long, deep and slow.
CHAKRA: 2
COLOR: Orange

MUDRA for Preventing BURNOUT

Living wild and living fast can have its price. Be who you are and enjoy every minute of it, but give your body enough down time to recover so that you can stay happy and healthy. This applies especially your non stop work ethics or extreme adventure sports. Know your limits and consciously assess the dangers and risks taken. A good approach is a planned even distribution of your energy and awareness of your stamina. Do not overexert yourself. This Mudra will help you preserve and recharge your vital energy.

Sit with a straight back. Bring your forearms up in front of you at heart level and bend your elbows to the side. With the palms facing the ground, fold your thumbs across the palms of each hand till they reach the bases of your ring fingers. Now bend your fingers slightly and touch the backs of your fingertips together, forming a V-shape with your hands. Hold for three minutes and make sure your elbows remain elevated.

BREATH: Long, deep and slow.
CHAKRA: 1, 2 ,3
COLOR: Red, yellow, orange

MANTRA: *OM*
(God in His Absolute State)

Scorpio

MUDRAS FOR LOVE

MUDRA for Sixth Chakra - TRUTH

In every love relationship honesty is a key component for harmony. Keeping secrets is limiting the level to which your love can grow. There is always a slight guard to keep and a distance is created. Give it a try and learn that when you are honest, you will enjoy the same quality in return. You are a mirror to your partner and everything that you see and do not like, you can find in yourself as well. The discontent that will overcome your relationship when you are burdened with secrets, may prove detrimental. This Mudra will help you overcome the tendency to "modify the truth" and truly feel free and merge with your partner.

Sit with a straight back. Bend your elbows and lift your arms up so that the elbows are parallel to the ground. Palms are facing out and all fingers are together. Hold for three minutes.

BREATH: Long, deep and slow.
CHAKRA: 6
COLOR: Violet

MANTRA: *EK ONG KAR*
(One Creator, God is One)

MUDRA FOR TRUST

The issue with trust is far from simple, but honestly answering this question may help: how much do you trust yourself? When you get jealous, suspicious and possessive, could it be possible that the situations you are connecting to your partner in reality apply to you? Do you have those habits? Could it be that knowing what you are capable of drives you mad and you are just venting? Here we are again back to honesty and truth. When you settle down and face your demons, know and understand why you have pursued something that may have jeopardized your true happiness at home, then the problem will vanish into the thin air. This Mudra will help you learn how to trust yourself and others. Most of all; trust the Divine power to always guide you into the right direction. Keep that channel clear.

Sit with a straight back. Make a circle with your arms arched up over your head, palms down. Put the right palm on top of the left. Lightly press the thumb tips together, keep your back straight and visualize a circle of white protective light around you.

BREATH: Short, fast, breath of fire focusing on the navel. Practice for a minute and relax with deep slow breath for another two minutes.

CHAKRA: 7
COLOR: Violet

MANTRA: *HAR HAR HAR WAHE GURU*
(God's Creation, His Supreme power and Wisdom)

MUDRA for POWERFUL SPEECH

Gentle words are soothing to the heart, healing the sorrow and nurturing to your lover. That is what we all desire to hear. Before you thoughtlessly say something you did not mean, take a breath and decide what is it you want to achieve as a result. If it is love and romance, then you, better than anyone, can create that sensual environment with words alone. If you want to hurt your lover in a stressful impulsive moment, take a step back and be wise. Each time you succumb to that urge, the love will be chipped away a bit. Not worth it, for your lover is yours alone. Be confident and communicate your passionate, powerful magnetism properly-with deeply profound love that you are capable of. This Mudra will help you remember how to embellish your words with seductive loving honey.

Sit with a straight back. Place your hands in front of your chest, palms apart and all fingertips touching. All fingers are spread apart. Inhale and press together the thumbs and the index fingers. Exhale and relax. Now inhale and press together the thumbs and the middle fingers. Exhale and relax. Continue the same way with the ring and little fingers. Practice for three minutes and finish up the cycle.

BREATH: Long, deep and slow.
CHAKRA: 5
COLOR: Blue

Scorpio

MUDRAS FOR SUCCESS

MUDRA for CALMING Your MIND

Your mind is on fire and the tendency can wear you out. You definitely have a competitive streak and when someone of the same profession near you does well, you will notice it and it will affect you. The best way to navigate this disposition is to use this a as stimulant to strive to get better and more successful. Remember that success comes in many ways and definitions and thoroughly reflect what is it really that you wish for. Be the master of your mind and you will become the master of your life. This Mudra will help you achieve the state of inner calm and peace. And that is an essential element for finding a balance and a successful, prosperous career.

Sit with a straight spine. Cross your arms in front of your chest, elbows are bend and at a ninety degree angle. Arms are parallel to the ground. Place the right palm on top of the left arm and the the top of the left hand under the right arm. All fingers are together and straight. Hold and keep the elbows nice and high.

BREATH: Long, deep and slow.
CHAKRA: 3, 4, 6
COLOR: Yellow, Green, indigo

MANTRA: *OM*
(God in His Absolute State)

MUDRA FOR WISDOM

Wise choices and wise decisions are part of the perfect plan to your success. Recognizing when something may not be the most positive experience for you and watching over your wild inner nature is what this Mudra will help you achieve. Make sure that your pursuits are motivated wisely and not just with pure emotion and passion. Use your intensity to magnify your natural power and there will be no limitations to what you can do and achieve. Inner wisdom can be awakened, heard and empowered when you wisely decide to do so. It is never too late or too early. The prefect time is now.

Sit with a straight spine and bend your elbows to the side, parallel to the ground. Make gentle fists, with the thumbs inside and the index fingers out. Now hook your index fingers around each other. The right palm is facing down and the left toward your chest.

BREATH: Long, deep and slow.
CHAKRA: 6
COLOR: Indigo

MANTRA: *SAT NAM*
(Truth Is God's Name, One in Spirit)

MUDRA for RELEASING Negativity

Your passionate nature can sometimes get dramatically discouraged when things don't go your way. But remember that every successful person failed many times before and certainly you would not want to give up. When you feel the competitive nature wallowing in jealousy if another person is winning, practice this Mudra and breathe out all that may not be positive. Consciously decide that all you want to carry around is positivity, love, passion, honesty and your immense inner power. Then you will become the true winner that you were born to be.

Sit with a straight back. Bend your arms and make fists with both hands. Bring them up in front of your heart. Cross the hands over each other, palms turned outwards. Hold the Mudra across the chest with the left arm on the outer side.

BREATH: Long, deep and slow.
CHAKRA: 4
COLOR: Green

Sagittarius

November 23 ~ December 21

BODY
Hips, thighs, liver

PLANET
Jupiter

COLORS
Dark blue, purple

ELEMENT
Fire

STONES and GEMS
Topaz

ANIMAL
Horse, deer

Sagittarius

MUDRAS FOR TRANSCENDING CHALLENGES

MUDRA OF GOOD SPEECH

You have the gift of understanding the mysterious and knowing the unknown. Often you find yourself in situations where you guide and teach others about life and old wisdom. It is therefore very important to avoid the unnecessary argument that may discredit the respect you enjoy. Using good tact and finding the best words when speaking and teaching others is essential. This Mudra will help you select and use words with eloquence for a powerful effect.

Sit with a straight back. Place your hands in front of your chest, palms apart and all fingertips touching. All fingers are spread apart. Inhale and press together the thumbs and the index fingers. Exhale and relax. Now inhale and press together the thumbs and the middle fingers. Exhale and relax. Continue the same way with the ring and little fingers. Practice for three minutes and finish up the cycle.

BREATH: Long, deep and slow.
CHAKRA: Throat 5
COLOR: Blue

MUDRA FOR PATIENCE

You move and think fast and expect the same of others. You can do many things at the same time and again naturally expect the same of others. That may be the reason why you are so impatient with others. Part of being a good teacher is the capacity to teach every single person no matter what level of knowledge they poses or how gifted they are. Teach with care, dedication, precise technique and certainly plenty of patience. Remember how time truly does not exist and you will get to see, do and experience everything you desire, all in due time. This Mudra will help you attain and develop the virtue of patience.

Sit with a straight spine. Make circles with the tips of your middle fingers and thumbs. Keep the rest of the fingers straight. Your upper arms are parallel to the floor and elbows are out to the sides. Your hands are at the level of your ears. Fingers are pointing towards the sky and palms are facing front. Hold for three minutes, breathe and keep the elbows nice and high.

BREATH: Long, deep and slow.
CHAKRA: 6, 7
COLOR: Indigo, white

MANTRA: *EK ONG KAR SAT GURU PRASAAD*
(One creator, Illuminated by God's Grace)

MUDRA FOR PREVENTING EXHAUSTION

When you feel passionate about something there is nothing that can stop you. You work on the project like you are running a marathon and rarely someone can catch up to you or match your perseverance. This is a great quality, but there may be a price with it. You could overextend yourself and then be forced to rest longer than the whole thing would have taken to accomplish, had you chosen a more human pace. Your other tendency to move from one project to next before the first one is completed, gives you a perpetual feeling of being in a hurry and that does not work to your advantage. This Mudra will help you balance your vital energy and prevent possible burnout.

Sit with a straight back, lift up your arms and grasp your earlobes with the thumb and index fingers. Hold your earlobes tightly and let the full weight of your arms pull on them. Relax and enjoy the immediate effects.

BREATH: Long, deep and slow.
CHAKRA: 3, 4
COLOR: Yellow, Green

MANTRA: *SAT NAM*
(Truth is God's Name, One in Spirit)

Sagittarius

MUDRAS FOR HEALTH AND BEAUTY

MUDRA FOR STRONG NERVES

Your enthusiastic and optimistic nature is something you love sharing with everyone around and near you. You are honest, straightforward and philosophical. That may take some time and effort when conveying to others. Not everyone is eager and ready to take on your jovial and good humored disposition and you will do everything in your power to convince them otherwise. This all takes a tremendous amount of energy which you do have, but let's face it, to be the cheering guide is a demanding proposition especially for your nerves. Learn how to protect, preserve, and nurture your nervous system with proper rest, diet and plenty of peaceful times where you can practice your spiritual meditative techniques. This Mudra is one of those to keep close and a regular part of your maintenance regimen.

Sit with a straight spine. Lift your left hand at ear level, palm facing out. Connect the thumb and middle finger and stretch out other fingers. Place your right hand in front of the solar plexus, palm facing up. The thumb and little finger are touching while other fingers are straight. **This position is reversed for men.**

BREATH: Long, deep and slow.
CHAKRA: 3, 4
COLOR: Yellow, green

MUDRA FOR RECHARGING

Your body seems indestructible and the never ending supply of energy that you pass onto others is magnetic. However, you are a human and need to be aware of your physical limitations. You are a natural sports enthusiast, remember that you need to adjust your tempo and demands on your body with time. Do not set over enthusiastic physical goals for yourself. Be tactful when setting limits. Another aspect that requires attention for your optimal health is a very smart diet plan. This will change with time as well, obviously when climbing Mount Everest your diet will differ from at-home holiday time. Recharge your body, mind, and spirit regularly with this Mudra and enjoy long lasting health thru all your adventures.

Sit with a straight spine. Extend your arms in front of you, parallel to the ground, keeping your elbows straight. Make a fist with your right hand and wrap the left hand around your right fist. The bases of the palms are touching and the thumbs are straight up. Hold for three minutes and relax.

BREATH: Long, deep and slow.
CHAKRA: 1, 2, 7
COLOR: Red, orange, violet

MUDRA for Preventing BURNOUT

Your sign rules the hips and thighs and you are often a gifted sportsman. You are spoiled by this indestructible natural gift especially in your youth and tend to take it for granted. Take the time now to preserve your splendid race-horse condition so that you may enjoy it for many years to come. Perhaps the challenges you set for yourself should be also more intellectual, which is a great stimulant and very important to you as well. This way, you will balance your energy levels and achieve much that you desire. This Mudra will help you harmonize your efforts and prevent burning out your power to quickly. Pace yourself.

Sit with a straight back. Bring your forearms up in front of you at heart level and bend your elbows to the side. With the palms facing the ground, fold your thumbs across the palms of each hand till they reach the bases of your ring fingers. Now bend your fingers slightly and touch the backs of your fingertips together, forming a V-shape with your hands. Hold for three minutes and make sure your elbows remain elevated.

BREATH: Long, deep and slow.
CHAKRA: 1, 2 ,3
COLOR: Red, yellow, orange

MANTRA: *OM*
(God in His Absolute State)

Sagittarius

MUDRAS FOR LOVE

MUDRA for OPENING Your HEART

Anyone who has ever been in love with you knows what an emotional puzzle you can be. Passionate, wild, and magnetic "soul mate" one moment and "no emotional demands" the next. Words like "always and forever" are banned from your vocabulary. You need your freedom like the air you breathe. However, if and when this phase which may last years, passes, you are ecstatic to settle down. First of all, just relax and let someone near. They won't bite and they won't chain you down. Just enjoy the moment and be. You may like it. This Mudra will help you open your heart and let the loved one in. This is the first step. The rest will follow.

Sit with a straight spine and lift your hands in front of your heart with palms and fingers open as if creating a cup. Keep all the fingers stretched and feel healing energy pouring into your fingertips and the area of your heart.

BREATH: Inhale long, deep and slow.
CHAKRA: 4
COLOR: Green

MANTRA: *SAT NAM*
(Truth is God's Name, One in Spirit)

MUDRA FOR FACING FEAR

As fearless as you are by nature there is one fear you need to conquer. The famous fear of commitment. Yes, you hate being cooped up inside, or committing to a schedule, but falling in love and "losing your freedom" petrifies you to death. It would be wise to relax and remember that you are only a prisoner in your mind where as in love, your power and freedom to conquer the world together is magnified many times over. With the right partner, you will realize that you are always free to fly the sky, but together you have someone special to enjoy the amazing view with. Relax, practice this Mudra and face this imaginary fear. Notice that there is no fear at all, it is just an idea of it. See, now you can breathe together and laugh. What joy.

Sit with a straight back. Bend your right elbow and lift the arm up to the level of your face. Face your palm outward, as if taking a vow. Bring your left arm in front of your navel, palm facing up. Concentrate on energy being received into your palms and hold for at least three minutes. Relax and be still.

BREATH: Long, deep and slow.
CHAKRA: 3, 7
COLOR: Yellow, violet

MANTRA: *NIRBHAO NIRVAIR AKAAL MORT*
(Fearless, Without Enemy, Immortal Personified God)

MUDRA for GUIDANCE

It has finally happened. You've fallen madly in love with your perfect match. What to do? The agony of feeling trapped and the million of other imaginary opportunities you are missing is maddening, but the power of love has taken over. Take some time for yourself and truly connect with your heart. It is love that you wanted and it is love that you got. You are lucky, fortunate and blessed. Now give it your very best effort and enjoy every single second of it. The social butterfly that you are, introduce your lover to your adventurous world and celebrate together. This Mudra will guide you thru this new experience. Every time you feel overwhelmed, practice this Mudra and receive guidance on how to proceed.

Sit with a straight spine. Place your hands together in front of your chest. Little fingers are pressed together to form a cup. Palms are facing towards the sky. Leave a very small opening between the sides of the little fingers. Gently focus your eyes towards the tip of your nose towards the palms. Have a clear question. Hold for three minutes, relax, be calm and wait for a clear answer.

BREATH: Long, deep and slow into your palms.
CHAKRA: 7
COLOR: White

Sagittarius

MUDRAS FOR SUCCESS

MUDRA FOR REJUVENATION

Your magnetic spirit will mesmerize others with your ideas and adventurous nature. You have the capacity to create excitement over a new project and gather a crowd of admirers. All that requires quite a stamina. Make it a regular part of your schedule to properly prepare for demanding events and occasions and "charge up" with Universal energy. After a successfully accomplished mission, take proper rest and relaxation where you can plan your next adventurous escapade and expand your philosophical views. You will need this Mudra to keep up with running in the race you've created.

Sit with a straight back. Place both palms of your hands directly on your ears. Circle your hands and massage your ears in a circular motion in the direction away from your face-counter clockwise. Listen to the sound of "*the ocean*" that you are creating with your hands.

BREATH: Long, deep and slow.
CHAKRA: 5, 6, 7
COLOR: Blue, indigo, violet

MANTRA: *OM*
(God in His Absolute State)

MUDRA FOR PROSPERITY

All that hard work, travel and teaching, but have you managed to deal with the proper pay back? Do not let your wild spirit ignore the realities and business matters. You must descend upon firm ground a few times a year and make sure that all is well and you know who is in charge of your affairs. You. Your wild nature has a bit of a tendency to be irresponsible and careless in financial matters. Your mission to the Moon costs quite a pretty penny, so make sure you don't return to the Earth dirt poor. This Mudra will help you attract, develop and maintain prosperity on all levels.

Sit with a straight back. Bring your hands in front of you, fingers together and palms facing down. Press the sides of the index fingers together and hold for a second. Now flip your hands over so that the palms are facing up toward the sky for a second and the edges of the little fingers are touching. Keep repeating and chant the mantra HAR with each change of hand position. Continue the practice for eleven minutes and rest.

BREATH: Short, fast breath of fire from the point of the navel, repeated with each mantra and Mudra movement.
CHAKRA: 1, 2, 3
COLOR: Red, orange, yellow

MANTRA: *HAR HAR*
(God, God)

MUDRA FOR MENTAL BALANCE

While you are ambitious on one hand, yet dislike discipline and schedule on the other, you will enjoy being your own boss and creating some unusual venture of your own. That does take inner discipline on your part and balance of your mind. Create a wise and well thought through business plan that envelops your intellectual and philosophical gifts and expands optimism among others. This Mudra will help you maintain that even mind so that you may pursue your colorful and unusual projects successfully, however you want to, and at your own pace.

Sit with a straight spine. Place your hands at solar plexus level in front of you and interlace the fingers backward with palms facing up. Fingers are pointing up and the thumbs are straight.

BREATH: Long, deep and slow.
CHAKRA: All
COLOR: All

MANTRA: *GOBINDAY, MUKUNDAY, UDAARAY, APAARAY, HARYNG, KARYNG, NIRNAMAY, AKAMAY*
(Sustainer, Liberator, Enlightener, Infinite, Destroyer, Creator, Nameless, Desireless)

Capricorn

December 22 ~ January 20

BODY
Knees, skin, bones, teeth

PLANET
Saturn

COLORS
Dark gray, black, dark brown

ELEMENT
Earth

STONES and GEMS
Turquoise, amethyst

ANIMAL
Goats

Capricorn

MUDRAS FOR TRANSCENDING CHALLENGES

MUDRA FOR OPENING YOUR CROWN

Your highly driven and hard working nature makes it challenging for you to sit still and go within. You will always get to the top of the mountain, but do remember that it is Divine Will that helped you get there as well as your hard work. Consciously connect and open your crown chakra and let the Universal Divine power nurture, rejuvenate and energize your being. It will be a relief to not always have to do everything yourself and on your own.   If you wish, keep your work associates at a distance, but get closer to the Universe-this connection will be always reliably helpful, and unconditionally loving.

Sit with a straight spine. Lift your hands above your head, all fingers kept apart as if you were holding a crown on your head. Keep the arms at this level and fingers stretched the entire practice. Visualize a stream of bright white light pouring into the crown of your head and filling your entire body with healing light.

BREATH: Long, deep and slow.
CHAKRA: 7
COLOR: VIOLET

MANTRA: *OM*
(God in His Absolute State)

MUDRA for RELEASING Negativity

When things don't instantly go your way, you might have a tendency to let the good feelings turn into pessimistic and cynical thought patterns. Maybe you are feeling responsible somewhere deep down for anything less than perfection. Be still and have a talk with yourself. Who's words are you listening to? Are they yours or maybe from your distant past? Release old pattern's and become free of anything that may be in the way of your vivacious and fun nature. Let your unusual sense of humor entertain you and make light of situation. Everything passes and it will do you good not to take yourself so seriously all the time. This Mudra will help you overcome this tendency and move into a brighter, more optimistic space.

Sit with a straight back. Bend your arms and make fists with both hands. Bring them up in front of your heart. Cross the hands over each other, palms turned outwards. Hold the Mudra across the chest with the left arm on the outer side.

BREATH: Long, deep and slow.
CHAKRA: 4
COLOR: Green

MUDRA FOR PROTECTION

You lead your close and extended family in addition to your business empire in every and each way and tend to forget to slow down a bit and pay attention to your inner deepest self. You are not alone in this world and even though sometimes your inner child feels forgotten amidst large crowds, remember that you are always protected and loved. Surround yourself with white healing light and practice this Mudra. Make it a part of your regular daily regimen, especially before demanding meetings or projects.

Sit with a straight spine. Cross your left hand over your right one and place them on your upper chest. Palms are facing you and all fingers are together. Hold for three minutes and feel the immediate energy shift.

BREATH: Long, deep and slow.
CHAKRA: All
COLOR: All

MANTRA: *OM*
(God Is His Absolute State)

Capricorn

MUDRAS FOR HEALTH AND BEAUTY

MUDRA for Protecting Your HEALTH

Being the hard worker and high achiever that you are, you need to pay just as much attention to keeping your body mind and soul fit, nurtured, healthy and fulfilled. This can not wait till tomorrow when you are fighting off the flu, tending to your family, launching a new project and helping a friend in need. The time is now and every day. First tend to yourself then you can take care of everyone else. Your executive carer positions usually require you to be in your office, so make extra effort to go out into nature where you can truly recharge your body, mind and spirit. It may not seem too practical at the time, but yes, it is worth it.

Sit with a straight back. Bend your right elbow and lift your left hand up, palm facing out. The index and middle fingers are pointing up; the rest are curled with the thumb over them. Hold your left hand in the same Mudra with the two stretched fingers touching your heart. Hold for three minutes.

BREATH: Inhale for ten counts, hold the breath for ten counts, and exhale for ten counts. Pace yourself comfortably, relax and be still.
CHAKRA: All color
COLOR: All color

MANTRA: *OM*
(God in His Absolute State)

MUDRA FOR ANTI AGING

We all know how some people tend to burn themselves out by working so hard it's like they are burning a candle at both ends. Well, you might be one of those people. Your ambition is a great asset and your disciplined nature will help you see any project thru, but you must not forget the essential element-yourself. What is an empire without a leader? So look at this as part of the practical must-do agenda. In order to preserve your youthful glow and recharge your battery, practice this Mudra and keep replenishing your being with everlasting power and indestructible stamina.

Sit with a straight back and make circles with your thumbs and index fingers. Stretch out the other fingers and place your hands on your knees, or in front of you-palms facing up.

BREATH: Short, fast breath of fire, focusing on the navel.
CHAKRA: 1, 2
COLOR: Red, orange

MANTRA: *EK ONG KAR SA TA NA MA*
(One Creator of Infinity, Birth, Death, and Rebirth)

MUDRA FOR STRONG NERVES

Even though you seem to be made of steel, your nerves are delicate and your skin sensitive. Keeping your nerves strong is essential for your health. Do not let all the responsibility and ambition deplete your reservoir of power. Your especially vulnerable areas of knees, bones and teeth need to be guarded as well. Over-extending your workload could cause injury or over loaded nervous system. This Mudra will help you preserve, protect and maintain healthy nerves.

Sit with a straight spine and lift your left hand to ear level with palm facing out. Connect the thumb and the middle finger while keeping the other fingers straight. The right hand is in your lap with thumb and little finger touching palm facing up towards the sky. The rest of the fingers are stretched. **The position is REVERSED for men.**

BREATH: Inhale long, deep and slow thru your nose in four counts,
and exhale in one strong breath.
CHAKRA: 3, 4
COLOR: Yellow, Green

Capricorn

MUDRAS FOR LOVE

MUDRA FOR LOVE

You like to be in control and falling in love is not one of those things. Suddenly you fell powerless and not the decision maker. Try to not interfere with your heart's journey, and take just as much time for developing the capacity to let it all happen naturally. You can not be in charge all the time. Relax and let love. Consciously get to a place of deep relaxation where you can soften up your invisible barriers and allow the transformative experience of falling in love happen. It may take an additional aspect like intellectual attraction, but love has to have a chance to breathe, grow and transform you. That is all part of the human experience. Allow this Mudra to show you the way.

Sit with a straight spine and raise your hands to the either side of your head. Curl the middle and ring fingers into your palm an extend the thumbs, index fingers, and little fingers. Keep your elbows from sinking and hold for three minutes.

BREATH: Inhale for eight short counts, with one strong, long exhale.
CHAKRA: 4
COLOR: Green

MANTRA: *SAT NAM WAHE GURU*
(God is Truth, His Is the Supreme Power and Wisdom)

MUDRA FOR RELEASING GUILT

There is a slightly controlling streak in your nature. When things do not go according to your envisioned plan, you try to change them to fit your picture. But manipulating anything in the matters of the heart has a high price. Look at love as a beautiful budding flower. You can not decide when it will bloom. Give it some air, sunshine, food, and love and enjoy the journey. Release the need for feeling responsible for everything and any feelings of guilt that arise when all does not go according to your fantastic plan. There is a better one already written. This Mudra will help you release any feelings of guilt and find that inner calmness you long for. Make space for pure, unconditional, and carefree love.

Sit with a straight back, elbows out to the sides, and bring your palms up to the level between your stomach and heart center. Palms are facing up toward the sky, right hand resting in left. Upper arms are slightly away from the body. Breathe slowly and deeply.

BREATH: Long, deep and slow.
CHAKRA: 3
COLOR: Yellow

MANTRA: *I AM THINE WAHE GURU*
(I am Thine, Divine Teacher within)

MUDRA FOR INNER SECURITY

When you feel insecure in matters of the heart, it is certain that both partners in relationship will pay the price. But remember, no one expects perfection and you are loved just the way you are. The other fact is that while you are quite independent yourself, you need a strong and secure partner at your side. When you want a confident partner, you need to first become one yourself. As you will learn, your carer success has little to do with confidence in matters of the heart. These are two different worlds. Let go of your reserved disposition and prudent inclinations. Just breathe and be free of everything you think you should be. For your lover, all you need to do is just show up. The rest will happen on its own.

Sit with a straight back, place your hands in reversed prayer pose: hands touching back to back at the level of your heart and solar plexus. Hold the pose for one and a half minutes, then repeat with the palms pressed together in a prayer pose.

BREATH: Long, deep and slow.
CHAKRA: 3, 4
COLOR: Yellow, green

MANTRA: *AD SHAKTI AD SHAKTI*
(I Bow to the Creator's Power)

Capricorn

MUDRAS FOR SUCCESS

MUDRA FOR RELAXATION AND JOY

All that hard work and running families as well as companies will mean nothing if you forget to enjoy it as well. Take a deep breath, stop for a moment and enjoy all that you've created. Being practical does not mean that relaxation is off limits. As a matter of fact, without experiencing some joy for all your efforts and hard work, your life will become very monotone and you will wonder why you feel so dissatisfied. And when you finally go on that long overdue vacation, do not book it solid with activities. Book it solid with nothing but air and laughter. Yes, you can be proud of yourself. Smile.

Sit with a straight back, lift up your hands up in front of your chest. Make a fist with your left hand, tucking the thumb inside. Wrap the right hand around the left and place your right thumb over the base of the left thumb. Concentrate on your third Eye area and hold for three minutes. Later, extend your practice to eleven minutes.

BREATH: Long, deep and slow.
CHAKRA: 3, 4
COLOR: Yellow, green

MANTRA: *HAREE HAR HAREE HAR*
(God in His Creative Aspect)

MUDRA for Higher CONSCIOUSNESS

While you are leading your tribe upward and onward, stop to take a break and know that you will become even a better leader-if that is at all possible-when you tune into your higher consciousness. Infusing some spirituality into your projects would be most important. On the other hand, do not go into the extreme opposite direction and fall into a lazy haze. Finding that perfect balance is the key. No matter what direction you turn, your success will reach new heights if you expand your consciousness and infuse some true otherworldliness into everything you do. This Mudra will help you connect to the ultimate power- your higher consciousness. With clear higher intention you can guide the world to be a better place.

Sit with a straight back. Put your palms together and extend your elbows to either side. Lift your hands in front of your heart, fingers pointed away from you. Each thumb is on the fleshy mound below the little finger of the same hand. Put the palms together with the right thumb snugly above the left thumb. The bottoms of the hands touch firmly. Hold the hands a few inches away from the body.

BREATH: Long, deep and slow.
CHAKRA: 3, 7
COLOR: Blue, violet

MANTRA: *OM*
(God in His Absolute State)

MUDRA for CREATIVITY

With all that ambition comes responsibility and the need for creative resolutions and endless ideas. How important it is to keep them coming, you know better than anyone else. Do not let your practical side overwhelm you, instead employ your tremendous capacity for patience and discipline. We all know that creativity is not just a simple button you can push and deliver a masterpiece. You do need to go into another consciousness and tap into the Source. Then your creative talents will deliver and all the pieces of the puzzle will come together. This Mudra will help keep your creativity flowing, growing and inspiring others. Also it will help you juggle your schedule - fitting for ten people-that only you are capable of maintaining.

Sit with a straight spine. Connect the thumbs and index fingers, keeping the rest of the fingers straight. Bend your elbows and lift your hands to your sides with palms facing up at a sixty-degree angle to your body. Concentrate on your Third eye and meditate for at least three minutes.

BREATH: Short, fast breath of fire from the navel.
CHAKRA: 6, 7
COLOR: Indigo, violet

MANTRA: *GA DA*
(God)

MUDRAS for AQUARIUS

Aquarius

January 21 ~ February 18

BODY
Ankles, circulation, skin

PLANET
Uranus & Saturn

COLORS
Violet, Aquamarine, Turquoise

ELEMENT
Air

STONES and GEMS
Blue sapphire, Amethyst, Aquamarine

ANIMAL
Large Birds

Aquarius

MUDRAS FOR TRANSCENDING CHALLENGES

MUDRA OF DIVINE WORSHIP

It is no secret that you want to save the world and every living specimen in it. You sense and feel what the future will bring and are perpetually ahead of your time. Your incredibly busy mind is working overtime on all channels. Before you become completely overwhelmed with various rescuing missions, remember there is a Universal guiding source that protects each and every one of us, including you. Connect with that source on a daily basis and your load will lighten considerably. After all, you are supposed to enjoy life as well.

Sit with a straight back, place both palms together in front of your chest. Concentrate on your breath and gently focus your gaze on your Third eye.

BREATH: Long, deep and slow.
CHAKRA: ALL
COLOR: ALL

MANTRA: *EK ONG KAR*
(One Creator, God is One)

MUDRA FOR TRUST

It is true that you may have the capacity to get things done faster that the rest of us, but that does not mean you have to do everything yourself. Be open to receiving help, it will help you focus on things of most importance that truly only you can accomplish. It is not easy to trust others with your heart driven projects, but you should be able to trust the Universe that it will guide you on your mission and will bring you others who are of the same energy and heart. Trusting the Universe is as important as every breath you take. So relax and practice this Mudra, and feel the pressure disappear with each breath.

Sit with a straight back, lift up your arms and create a circle with arms arched above head. Palms are turned down, women place right palm over left, men left palm over right. The thumb tips are pressed together lightly. Close your eyes and visualize a protective circle of white healing light all around you.

BREATH: Fast breath of fire from the point of your navel.
CHAKRA: 7
COLOR: Violet

MANTRA: *HAR HAR HAR WAHE GURU*
(God's Creation, His Supreme Power and Wisdom)

MUDRA FOR EMPOWERING YOUR VOICE

As a born peacemaker you are well aware of the importance and power of words. Your diplomatic speaking talents are under constant scrutiny and pressure. You need to be able to concentrate with ease, so you can get to the point in the shortest time possible, before the peace talks time expires and everyone's attention is gone. This Mudra will help you speak with power and conviction so that you will successfully project your message to a wide audience and accomplish your mission.

Sit with a straight back, bend your elbows and lift them parallel to the ground, while you lift your hands in front of you at the level of your throat. Turn the right palm outward and the left palm towards you. Bend your fingers and hook them together, while pulling them apart. Keep your shoulders down while applying pressure to the pull.

BREATH: Long deep and slow.
CHAKRA: 5
COLOR: Blue

Aquarius

MUDRAS FOR HEALTH AND BEAUTY

MUDRA FOR PREVENTING EXHAUSTION

You rarely allow yourself the time for rest and relaxation, and now it is time to do just that. Your vulnerable area of ankles may get accident prone if you are exhausted and keep going without a break. Take care and caution and do not overextend yourself. Make regular time for letting go and replenishment of your strong physical energy battery. This Mudra will create a perfect opportunity for "hands on" relaxation and a much needed break.

Sit with a straight back, lift up your arms and grasp your earlobes with the thumb and index fingers. Hold your earlobes tightly and let the full weight of your arms pull on them. Relax and enjoy the immediate effects.

BREATH: Long, deep and slow.
CHAKRA: 3, 4
COLOR: Yellow, Green

MANTRA: *SAT NAM*
(Truth is God's Name, One in Spirit)

MUDRA for UPLIFTING Your HEART

Being that you are such an active thinker, sometimes presents a challenge. You forget about yourself. Try to remember the health of your heart is important as well. The reality is, that you can not always save everyone. This world is a learning experience and everyone needs to go thru it at some time or another. And while you understand this, you do not like it and in brings you unhappiness. This Mudra will help you uplift your heart, so that you may masterfully find the perfect balance of mind and heart. This way, when you successfully accomplish a challenging project, you will actually recognize it, and feel happy in your heart as well. Tomorrow is another day.

Sit with a straight back, elbows bend and parallel to the ground. Tuck your thumbs under your armpits and keep the rest of your fingers straight and together, palms facing down. The middle finger fingertips are touching, but with each inhale they separate, while with each inhale they touch or cross each other. Focus on expanding your chest and opening your heart area.

BREATH: Long, deep and slow.
CHAKRA: 4
COLOR: Green

MUDRA FOR STRONG NERVES

The high responsibilities that you carry is a scenario that you create, are capable of seeing thru, and actually enjoy, but you must remember that your nervous system can suffer consequences of overload. This can result in nervous sensitivity and skin ailments. Make an effort to relax your schedule a bit, take a break, and take care of your basic needs like sleep, diet and complete relaxation. To prevent a work overload and suffer consequences, practice this Mudra and preserve your nerves. You have many goals and projects to accomplish, so pace yourself and protect your health assets. You will se what a difference it will make if you replenish your energy and take a few steps back. With some distance and air, your mind will be even more in tune. They sky is the limit.

Sit with a straight spine and lift your left hand to ear level with palm facing out. Connect the thumb and the middle finger while keeping the other fingers straight. The right hand is in your lap with thumb and little finger touching palm facing up towards the sky. The rest of the fingers are stretched. **The position is REVERSED for men.**

BREATH: Inhale long, deep and slow thru your nose in four counts and exhale in one strong breath.
CHAKRA: 3, 4
COLOR: Yellow, Green

Aquarius

MUDRAS FOR LOVE

MUDRA FOR PATIENCE

Yes, you may know at first glance when you meet the love of your life, but not everyone is that fast. You may frighten your love away, if you come bulldozing in-full-force and are ready to elope within five minutes of meeting. Be tactful with your words and do not reveal your heart immediately. If you do, it may take your conquest a few weeks to recover and find the courage for the next date with you. By then you will have suffered thru massive frustration. Be patient and considerate. This Mudra will help you ease and tame your impatient nature and redirect your energy into a calmer more productive approach. You may jump into water fast, but take a nice easy swim first before you take over the sailboat and kidnap it for life.

Sit with a straight back, lift your hands up to shoulder level and keep elbows nice and high – level with the shoulders. Connect the thumbs and the middle fingers on both hands and stretch the rest of the fingers. Your hands are at the level of your ears, palms facing out and fingers nice and stretched towards the sky.

BREATH: Long, deep and slow.
CHAKRA: 6,7
COLOR: Indigo, White

MANTRA: *EK ONG KAR SAT NAM GURU PRASAAD*
(One creator, Illuminated by God's Grace)

MUDRA for OPENING Your HEART

When you are dealing with the matters of love, it is time to redirect your intense focus and open your heart to show the softer, gentler side of your personality. Infuse some of that energy in your work when saving the world and nature and your will attract a more loving crowd of supporters. When communicating with your lover, melt into the softie that you are and expose your vulnerable side as well. Otherwise they will completely miss that quality in you, and fear that you are cold-hearted when in fact your mind is just intensely greedy for your attention. Your heart needs to take center-stage position, and the time is now.

Sit with a straight spine and lift your hands in front of your heart with palms and fingers open as if creating a cup. Keep all the fingers stretched and feel the healing energy pouring into your fingertips and the area of your heart.

BREATH: Long, deep and slow.
CHAKRA: 4
COLOR: Green

MANTRA: *SAT NAM*
(Truth is God's Name, One in Spirit)

MUDRA OF TWO HEARTS

It is not easy to love such an independent and freedom loving person as yourself. But each love relationship involves both people and it is important that you remember this. So when you make an unexpected plan to run alone and free along the ocean for a bit, it would be wise to inform your lover. They will still love you, but it will help them understand that your excursion has nothing to do with them, you just needed some fresh air. That way, there will be no hurt feelings and nothing to explain later and you will have the feeling or air and free space between you two, even though you are inseparably madly in love. By being considerate, you will have a good chance to enjoy this earthly love, not just the "out of this world" wild fantasy that you dream about. You are here in this world right now, so might as well enjoy earthly love. You can visit other planets another time.

Sit with a straight spine. Connect the thumbs and index fingers on each hand and spread out and extend all other fingers. Lift your arms in front of your heart, cross arms in front of you - left in front of right, palms facing out and little fingers hooked onto each other. Keep fingers nice and extended thru the practice.

BREATH: Inhale long, deep and slow.
CHAKRA: 4
COLOR: Green

MANTRA: *SAT NAM*
(Truth is God's Name, One in Spirit)

Aquarius

MUDRAS FOR SUCCESS

MUDRA FOR CONCENTRATION

You enjoy tremendous satisfaction when your efforts are rewarded, and you can see the fruits of your hard labor. However, your creative ideas run so wild that it is essential for you to be able to focus and concentrate on one specific area at a time. Become a true Aquarian master of the oceans and know how to navigate the waters of your wild inner oceans of creativity and invention. This Mudra will help you achieve a high level of concentration, while keeping your eye on the target.

Sit with a straight back. Curl each index into the thumbs and stretch the other fingers. Bring your hands up above navel area and place the backs of palms together-back to back. Palms are facing out. Keep the stretched fingers pointed up towards the sky and feel the stretch in your wrist and palm area.

BREATH: Long, deep and slow.
CHAKRA: 3, 4, 6
COLOR: Yellow, Green, violet

MANTRA: *AKAL AKAL AKAL HARI AKAAL*
(Immortal Creator)

MUDRA FOR A SHARP MIND

Multi tasking is a fun past time for you and you love to juggle a multitude of projects at once. However, you are still human and sometimes your brain can go into overdrive. Learn to experience different phases of your creative spells. The proper distance is required sometimes to observe the project from a different perspective. This will prove very valuable. During those rare quiet moments of reflection, practice this Mudra. It will help you maintain a razor sharp edge and stay ahead of the curve, which is where you feel right at home and in your comfort zone.

Sit with a straight spine. Hold the left hand up in front of you chest as if ready to clap, then with an extended index and middle finger of your right hand firmly walk up the center of the left palm, starting at the bottom of the palm and continuing to the very tips of middle and ring fingers of the left hand. Walk up and down your palm while maintaining pressure.

BREATH: Long, deep and slow.
CHAKRA: 3, 6
COLOR: Yellow, Indigo

MANTRA: *HARA HARE HARI*
(The Creator in Action)

MUDRA FOR BALANCING THE YIN AND YANG

Do not get discouraged if others can't follow your world-saving actions quite as fast as you would like. Every flower needs time to grow, push a bud and then finally bloom in full glory. Be aware that this world is full of contradictions and opposites, and remember that with your determined vision and devoted purpose for a better world, you will see it thru with patience and in harmony with everyone and everything. Perhaps during a moment of apparent set-back you will be gifted with another element that will truly infuse your work with magic. This will bring you immense sense of fulfillment, purpose and destiny.

Sit with a straight spine. Connect the index and thumb fingers and extend the rest of the fingers. Lift your right hand in front of your chest with palm turned out and hold the left hand below in front of your stomach area, palm turned inward. Connect the thumbs and index fingers of both hands creating the Wheel of life.

BREATH: Long, deep and slow.
CHAKRA: All
COLOR: All

MANTRA: *OM*
(God in His Absolute State)

MUDRAS for PISCES

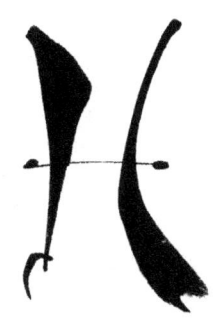

Pisces

February 19 ~ March 20

BODY
Feet

PLANET
Neptune

COLORS
Soft sea green

ELEMENT
Water

STONES and GEMS
Moonstone, bloodstone

ANIMAL
Fish, mammals in water

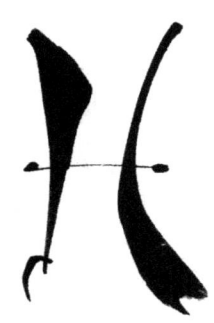

Pisces

MUDRAS FOR TRANSCENDING CHALLENGES

MUDRA for RELAXATION and JOY

There is a wonderful giving and caring quality in you. You love to help others and often completely forget about yourself in the process. But there are times when you need to escape into your own world. You will leave everyone hanging and believing that you disappeared from the face of the earth when in fact you are just hiding at home. Or you may go to a far away land without much ado. When regular life circumstances prevent you from that complete escape, you can create a quick joy trip with the practice of this Mudra. It does not matter where you are, you can find the same inner joy that you experienced in Tibet or the Maldives in your very own backyard.

Sit with a straight back, lift up your hands up in front of your chest. Make a fist with your left hand, tucking the thumb inside. Wrap the right hand around the left and place your right thumb over the base of the left thumb. Concentrate on your Third eye area and hold for three minutes. Later, extend your practice to eleven minutes.

BREATH: Long, deep and slow.
CHAKRA: 3, 4
COLOR: Yellow, green

MANTRA: *HAREE HAR HAREE HAR*
(God in His Creative Aspect)

MUDRA for OVERCOMING ADDICTIONS

Your intense nature can sometimes seduce you into an extreme situation. You love escaping reality and living in your dreams. You may get addicted to that dream escapist life. Don't get lost and forget why you are here in this world. You are meant to nurture and elevate your gift of extra sensory perception to help yourself and others experience a fuller and happier life. When your willpower is weak and you feel you could be easily led, pay special attention and avoid vulnerable situations. Take some time away from disruptive circumstances or people and find your inner power and remember your goals. Writing and being creative may be a fantastic outlet for you and perhaps you may take an acting class where you can pretend to be anyone you wish. This Mudra will help you stay on right track no matter where you find yourself. Stay focused.

Sit with a straight back. Make fists with both hands and then extend the thumbs out. Press the thumbs on the temples where you feel a slight depression. Clench your teeth, lock the back molars, and keep your lips closed. Vibrate the jaw muscles by alternating the pressure on the molars. A muscle will move in rhythm under the thumbs. Feel it massage the thumbs as you continue to apply firm pressure with them. Concentrate on your third eye center as you do this. Continue for three to eleven minutes. Now relax your arms and place them at your sides, with the thumbs and index fingers forming a circle. Hold and relax.

BREATH: Long, deep and slow.
CHAKRA: 1, 2, 3, 4, 5
COLOR: Red, orange, yellow, green, blue

MUDRA for Calling the GODS of Earth

You love to dream and live in your own fantasy land. The reality of this world may be too much for your super intuitive and psychic spirit. You wish you could disappear and live where everything is different - otherworldly. But, you are here now and there are angels to help you on this plane of existence too. Call the Gods of this sacred world and learn that all life here on Earth, all lands and all people have a spark of love and beauty in them. Practice this Mudra when you need to reconnect with the power of Earth and feel it's powerful healing and recharging energy. Go into nature, breathe, and just be.

Sit with a straight back. Bend your elbows and place your left hand at your solar plexus, palm facing upward, fingers together. Bring your right hand below your left, palm facing your body, and point the right index finger down toward the Earth.

BREATH: Long, deep and slow
CHAKRA: 1, 7
COLOR: Red, violet

MANTRA: **OM** (God in His Absolute State)

Pisces

MUDRAS FOR HEALTH AND BEAUTY

MUDRA for Preventing BURNOUT

Your sign rules the feet so take especially good care of them. Pamper yourself, enjoy moments of relaxation and rest, and learn to choose between unnecessary obligations, promises, and your duty to take care of your own health and body above all the rest. Do not wait until it's is too late and your body forces you to be still. Train your mind to give your body a well deserved break. When you need to push the "reset" button and recharge, practice this Mudra and enjoy the powerful effects of immediate calm and serene energy that will envelop you. Make it a point to practice anytime you feel yourself overly extending and protect your health.

Sit with a straight back. Bring your forearms up in front of you at heart level and bend your elbows to the side. With the palms facing the ground, fold your thumbs across the palms of each hand till they reach the bases of your ring fingers. Now bend your fingers slightly and touch the backs of your fingertips together, forming a V-shape with your hands. Hold for three minutes and make sure your elbows remain elevated.

BREATH: Long, deep and slow.
CHAKRA: 1, 2 ,3
COLOR: Red, yellow, orange

MANTRA: *OM*
(God in His Absolute State)

MUDRA for HEALING Your HEART Chakra

You are extremely sensitive to outside sensory stimuli and even a spell of bad weather can send you into a different zone. Your emotional nature is susceptible to the smallest changes and your heart is easily hurt. Practice compassion for yourself as well and take precious care of your sensitive constitution. Create some special time for your inner harmony and peace. Enjoy a few silent minutes every day, listen to your heart and your soul. Heal any wounds or little hurts that you may carry and prepare for new, happy life's adventures. This Mudra will help you preserve and maintain a vibrant heart center.

Sit with a straight spine. Lift your right hand up, elbow bent, your hand at the level of your face. Make a fist and leave only the index finger extended, pointing up. Place your left hand on your chest above your breast, elbow parallel to the ground. Hold and feel the energy shifting in your body. Keep the elbows nice and high.

BREATH: Long, deep and slow.
CHAKRA: 4
COLOR: Green

MUDRA FOR INVISIBILITY

You are quite famous for your disappearing act and you are right to do so. When you finally give yourself permission to rest-you vanish. However, wouldn't you like to achieve the same effect by making yourself practically invisible no matter where you are? Just block other people's invasive or energy draining habit, protect yourself with a shield of invisibility and practice this Mudra. Learn to observe the world around you and enjoy being unnoticed or looked right thru-just like cellophane. You are untouchable, unbeatable and invisible. Now breathe, and completely relax.

Sit with a straight spine and make a fist with your right hand. Lift it to the level of your solar plexus, the palm facing toward you. Now hold your left hand above your right fit, palm facing down. The hands are not touching. Hold for three minutes and relax.

BREATH: Long, deep and slow.
CHAKRA: All
COLOR: All

MANTRA: *OM*
(God in His Absolute State)

Pisces

MUDRAS FOR LOVE

MUDRA FOR FACING FEAR

You are such and idealist that there might be a time when you experience a rude awakening once the rose glasses come off, and you see that your perfect partner may not be perfect at all. However, this will only enable and prepare you for the right time-the right person where you can build up the relationship on firm ground. But after a first hard learned lesson, you know you are guarding your heart and are afraid to have someone play with your feelings again. You may not feel secure enough within yourself to jump into "the unknown waters of love " again, even though you are a great swimmer. Every fear is only big until you face it and then it dwindles into thin air. It's all a part of life experience. This Mudra will help you become fearless.

Sit with a straight back. Bend your right elbow and lift the arm up to the level of your face. Face your palm outward, as if taking a vow. Bring your left arm in front of your navel, palm facing up. Concentrate on energy being received into your palms and hold for at least three minutes. Relax and be still.

BREATH: Long, deep and slow.
CHAKRA: 3, 7
COLOR: Yellow, violet

MANTRA: *NIRBHAO NIRVAIR AKAAL MORT*
(Fearless, Without Enemy, Immortal Personified God)

MUDRA FOR HAPPINESS

When your "lucky in love" moment finally arrives, you are faced with your next challenge: letting go enough so that you can actually enjoy your love. In matters of the heart you are so sensitive, that anything could sweep you into an overly emotional state. You express your affection generously and your partner could be overwhelmed with all you have to give. The key is not to worry, and know that they are happy simply just by being with you. So relax, and remember that happy moments are the simplest, most natural and unplanned, the less you wonder where it is, the faster it is going to come your way. Take a deep breath and know that this precise moment in time is the absolute happiness you have been waiting for. All is well and life is great.

Sit with a straight spine. Bend your elbows and bring your arms to your sides, away from your body. Elbows are just below the level of the shoulders. Palms are facing forward. Stretch the index and middle fingers and bend the ring and little fingers, pressing them into the palms firmly with the thumbs. Hold for three minutes and relax.

BREATH: Long, deep and slow.
CHAKRA: 4
COLOR: Green

MANTRA: *SAT NAM*
(Truth is God's Name, One in Spirit)

MUDRA FOR BALANCING THE YIN AND YANG

Yes, it is true: nobody is perfect and not even you. The great truth is stored deep inside your soul and you know that your super sensitivity can sometimes be equaled with complete careless and rude behavior. This will leave your counterpart confused and upset. You are the most romantic lover and then suddenly you may disappear without a sound into your mysterious seclusion. Your loved one is left wondering how could the most otherworldly dream disappear so quickly. To help balance and admit to who you are-two fish swimming in opposite directions-practice this Mudra and prepare your lover for your 180 degree spin. Then the unpredictable becomes just a small spell of your sensitivity and all is understood and harmonious.

Sit with a straight spine. Connect the index and thumb fingers and extend the rest of the fingers. Lift your right hand in front of your chest with palm turned out and hold the left hand below in front of your stomach area, palm turned inward. Connect the thumbs and index fingers of both hands creating the Wheel of life.

BREATH: Long, deep and slow.
CHAKRA: All
COLOR: All

MANTRA: *OM*
(God in His Absolute State)

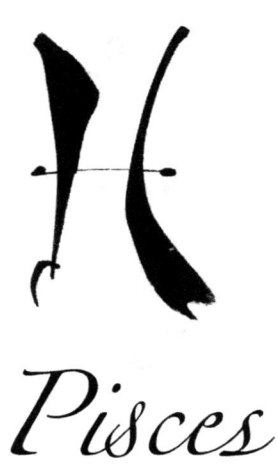

Pisces

MUDRAS FOR SUCCESS

MUDRA for OPENING Your CROWN

To let your natural ability for artistry in whatever profession you choose flow freely through you undisturbed, empower yourself with this Mudra. It will help you magnify the creative power that surrounds your entire being. Ask for guidance and direction where and how to channel your power. Be still and listen to your inner voice patiently. Your own answer will guide you. You will become the pure channel of creative manifestation, a rare gift and endless treasure of imagination, phantasy and fascinating otherworldliness. This is your special gift that can bring you much success.

Sit with a straight spine. Lift your hands above your head, all fingers kept apart as if you were holding a crown on your head. Keep the arms at this level and fingers stretched the entire practice. Visualize a stream of bright white light pouring into the crown of your head and filling your entire body with healing light.

BREATH: Long, deep and slow.
CHAKRA: 7
COLOR: VIOLET

MANTRA: *OM*
(God in His Absolute State)

MUDRA FOR CONCENTRATION

If you feel your two Pisces aspects swimming in different directions, become still, practice this Mudra and concentrate. When it comes to your career, this is not the place to be too emotional, feel sorry for yourself, or indulge in self pity. Remember that every successful person failed many times before and so shall you. After a few persistent tries, you will succeed in your deepest dreams. But this does require concentration, hard work, plan and action-not just daydreaming the final outcome. Visualize every step of the way and practice succeeding in your mind. When the moment arrives you will be ready. Now that all is accomplished, you should try to enjoy your hard earned success. Be in the moment.

Sit with a straight back. Curl each index into the thumbs and stretch the other fingers. Bring your hands up above navel area and place the backs of palms together-back to back. Palms are facing out. Keep the stretched fingers pointed up towards the sky and feel the stretch in your wrist and palm area.

BREATH: Long, deep and slow.
CHAKRA: 3, 4, 6
COLOR: Yellow, Green, violet

MANTRA: *AKAL AKAL AKAL HARI AKAAL*
(Immortal Creator)

MUDRA FOR TRUST

Ah, the big unknown word...trust. The key to conquering this particular challenge is answering a very important question: do you trust yourself? You will attract into your life what you project into the world, so remember how powerful every though and word you say is. Trust that with right intentions, you will find a way. Trust that when you are on the right path, doors will open. Trust that the perfect people will come your way to help you get where you need to go. Trust that you will accomplish your mission, if you put your heartfelt passion and intention into it. Trust that if something does not work out, a much better opportunity will present itself. Trust that you are always and every moment protected, watched over and very much loved. Always trust in that. This Mudra will help you develop and practice Trust.

Sit with a straight back. Make a circle with your arms arched up over your head, palms down. Put the right palm on top of the left. Lightly press the thumb tips together, keep your back straight and visualize a circle of white protective light around you.

BREATH: Short, fast, breath of fire focusing on the navel. Practice for a minute and relax with deep slow breath for another two minutes.

CHAKRA: 7
COLOR: Violet

MANTRA: *HAR HAR HAR WAHE GURU*
(God's Creation, His Supreme power and Wisdom)

About the Author

SABRINA MESKO Ph.D.H.

SABRINA MESKO Ph.D.H. is a recognized Mudra authority and International and Los Angeles Times bestselling author of the timeless classic *Healing Mudras - Yoga for your Hands* translated into fourteen languages, as well as twenty other books on Mudras, Mudra Therapy, Mudras and Astrology, and meditation techniques.

Sabrina was born in Europe where she became a classical ballerina at an early age. In her teens she moved to New York and became a principal Broadway dancer and singer who turned to yoga to heal a back injury. Eastern-trained but Western-based, she completed a several-year intensive study of teachings with world renowned Masters, one of whom entrusted her with bringing the sacred Mudra techniques to the West. She is a Yoga College of India certified Yoga Therapist.

Sabrina holds a Bachelors Degree in Sensory Approaches to Healing, a Masters in Holistic Science and a Doctorate in Ancient and Modern Sensory Approaches to Healing, in addition to a Ph.D.H in Healtheology from the American Institute of Holistic Theology. She is board certified from the American Alternative medical Association and American Holistic Health Association.

She has been featured in media outlets such as The Los Angeles Times, CNBC News, Cosmopolitan, the cover of London Times Lifestyle, The Discovery Channel documentary on Hands, W magazine, First for Women, Health, WebMD, Daily News, Focus, Yoga Journal, Australian Women's weekly, Blend, Daily Breeze, New Age, the Roseanne Show and various international live television programs. Her articles have been published in world-wide publications. She hosted her own weekly TV show educating about health, well-being and complementary medicine. She is an executive member of the World Yoga Council and has led numerous international Yoga Therapy educational programs. She directed and produced her interactive double DVD titled *Chakra Mudras* - a Visionary awards finalist. Sabrina also created award winning international Spa and Wellness Centers and is a motivational keynote conference speaker addressing large audiences all over the world. Sabrina recently launched Arnica Press, a boutique Book Publishing House. Her mission is to discover, mentor, nurture and publish unique authors with a meaningful message, that may otherwise not have an opportunity to be heard.

She is the founder of MUDRA MASTERY ™ the world's only online Mudra Teacher and Mudra Therapy Education, Certification, and Mentorship program, with her certified graduates and therapists spreading these ancient teachings in over 26 countries around the world.

WWW.SABRINAMESKO.COM

www.ingramcontent.com/pod-product-compliance
Lightning Source LLC
Chambersburg PA
CBHW081220170426
43198CB00017B/2668